WALKER'S COMPANION

—— WALES ——

WALKER'S COMPANION

WALES

FRANK DUERDEN
AND ROGER THOMAS

Photography by
John Heseltine and David Ward

WARD LOCK

ACKNOWLEDGMENTS

The authors would like to thank the following: **Snowdonia**: John Ellis Roberts; John Fox; Fred Taylor; Mr Hywel Roberts; Mr Alan Jones; Mr D. Archer; Miss M. Rees; Mr P.A. Ogden; officials of the Forestry Commission at Aberystwyth; the Nature Conservancy Council at Ffordd Penrhos; the National Trust at Llandudno; Mr R.J. Jones; the Snowdon Mountain Railway Company; Mr John Keylock; Mr H. Nicholls and Mr P. Abnett; Wm Collins Sons and Co. Ltd. (for extracts from *Wild Tales* by George Borrow); the Countryside Commission; the Ordnance Survey (for permission to draw the maps from Outdoor Leisure maps); the Snowdonia National Park Authority; Gwynedd County Council Planning Department; Miss Jacqueline Montague, Miss Patricia Webster, Mrs Jennifer Peck and my daughter, Sharon, who typed the manuscripts and my wife, Audrey, and daughter, Beverley, who helped me with the proofreading. **Brecon Beacons and Pembrokeshire:** Staff at the Brecon Beacons National Park and the Pembrokeshire Coast National Park; in particular, Roger Stevens, Alan Ward and their colleagues at Brecon, and George Yeomans at Haverfordwest; Elinor Gwynn; Colin Horsman, a friend and a fellow walker who gave me invaluable help with the Brecon Beacons routes; Jill Morgan and Greg Nuttgens. I cannot finish without a note of gratitude to my family: Liz, Huw and Oswain.

A WARD LOCK BOOK

First published in the UK 1995 by
Ward Lock, Villiers House, 41/47 Strand, London WC2N 5JE

A Cassell Imprint

Text © Frank Duerden and Roger Thomas 1995   Photographs © Ward Lock 1995

This book is based on material originally published in the *Great Walks* series.

A British Library Cataloguing in Publication Data block for this book may be obtained from the British Library

ISBN 0 7063 7349 9

Typeset by Litho Link Ltd, Welshpool, Powys, Wales
Printed and bound in Spain by Graficromo S.A., Cordoba

Contents

INTRODUCTION

Wales encompasses a great diversity of scenery and terrain and the walks included here are within the boundaries of its three National Parks. The immensely popular Snowdonia National Park was designated in 1951 and covers 838 sq miles (224,293 hectares), the second largest park after the Lake District. As well as the facilities provided by the Snowdonia National Park, the Forestry Commission has designated an area of almost 20,000 acres (9710 hectares) as the Snowdonia Forest Park. It was established in 1937 and consists of Gwydyr Forest, around Betws-y-Coed and Beddgelert Forest to the north-west of Beddgelert. It is an area of forest open to the public for recreation and generally the walker is free to use any path or forest road.

There are also sixteen National Nature Reserves, managed by the Nature Conservancy Council, in the Snowdonia National Park. A permit is *not* required to enter the Reserves mentioned in this book, but may be needed to obtain access to some of the others — these are available from the appropriate local regional office.

The Brecon Beacons form the nucleus of a National Park that came into existence in 1957, the last of Britain's ten parks. Although the park is named after the Brecon Beacons, the Beacons are only one of four mountain ranges within the park boundaries. Matters are further confused by the fact that two of the mountain ranges share almost identical names. The Brecon Beacon National Park actually consists of the borderland Black Mountains, the central Brecon Beacons, Fforest Fawr and the western Black Mountain (singular).

As far as the visitor to the area is concerned, by far the best introduction to the National Park is to be found at the Brecon Beacon Mountain Centre above the village of Libanus, open all year (see addresses). In addition there are Information Centres open seasonally at Abergavenny (01873 3254), Brecon (01874 4437) and Llandovery (01550 26093). The National Park is also responsible for the Craig-y-nos Country Park, open all year, near Abercraf (01639 730395) where an Information Point is manned in the summer months. The Park also runs the Danywenallt Study Centre, a residential field study centre at Aber, near Talybont-on-Usk (01874 87677).

The Pembrokeshire Coast National Park is unique. Designated in 1952, it is the smallest park at 225 sq miles (58,250 hectares) and is the only one to be coast-based. It is also the only predominantly lowland National Park in Britain, a characteristic responsible for further distinctive features. For example, Pembrokeshire has twice the average population density of the other parks, and a much more intensive pattern of agriculture. There is a network of Information Centres, open seasonally, at Newport (01239 820912), St Davids (01437 720392), Broad Haven (01437 781412), Pembroke (01646 682148), Haverfordwest (01437 66141), Tenby (01834 2402) and Kilgetty (01834 811411).

The walks take in the magnificent scenery of these areas, which varies from the wide open spaces, grassy hillsides, high plateaux and expansive moorlands of the Brecon Beacons in the south to the volcanic jumble, serrated skylines and intricate boulder strewn slopes of Snowdonia in the north. The stunning cliffs and superb stretches of untouched coastline of the Pembrokeshire coast are especially enjoyable in the spring when the wild flowers are out, the sea birds are everywhere to be seen, and the weather is normally kind.

With an aim of achieving a reasonable distribution of routes across the three National Parks, the walks cover a wide range of length and difficulty to appeal to as many walkers as possible and will suit those who are content to follow some of the easier routes along the valleys as well as those who wish to try some of the more ambitious routes up into the mountains.

Unfortunately, each year there are accidents and occasional deaths involving walkers. The more difficult walks are best attempted in reasonably good weather and a section on safety has been included, although in the end, safety precautions must be left to the judgement of the individual concerned.

The information given was accurate when collected, but inevitably time will erode its value. Fortunately, the route descriptions are likely to remain reasonably accurate. Where footpaths change, it is usually as the result of a deliberate diversion, for example to allow a badly eroded path to recover, and the diversion will usually be well marked. In such cases, of course, the diversion should always be followed.

INTRODUCTION TO THE ROUTE DESCRIPTIONS

1. ACCESS (see page 123) The routes described later have, as far as is known, been walked for a long time without objection and it is not expected therefore that any difficulties will be encountered. Nevertheless, they do in some cases cross country over which there is, strictly speaking, no legal right of way, and in such cases the responsibility must lie with the walker to obtain any necessary permission before crossing such land. In particular, 'short cuts' should not be taken that could cause annoyance to local people.

2. ASCENT The amount of climbing involved in each route has been estimated from Outdoor Leisure or 1:50 000 maps as appropriate and should be regarded as approximate only. The nature of the coastal terrain in Pembrokeshire makes ascent information irrelevant.

3. CAR-PARKS The nearest public car-park is given. There will be many places where a car can be parked by the wayside, but it must be done with care, as indiscriminate parking can be a great nuisance to local people.

4. INTERESTING FEATURES The best position for seeing these is indicated both in the route descriptions and on the maps by (1), (2), etc.

5. LENGTH These are strictly 'map miles' estimated from the Outdoor Leisure maps; no attempt has been made to take into account any ascent or descent involved.

6. MAPS The maps are drawn to a scale of approximately 1:25 000 (see page 10) and all names are as given on the Outdoor Leisure maps. Field boundaries in particular should be taken as a 'best description'. The maps have been drawn in the main, so that the route goes from the bottom to the top of a page. This will enable the reader to 'line up' the map whilst still holding the book in the normal reading position. The arrow on each map points to grid north. The scale of some small features has been slightly exaggerated for clarity. For easy cross-reference the relevant Outdoor Leisure and Landranger sheets are indicated.

FIGURE 1 The approximate starting points of the routes

The letters 'L' and 'R' stand for left and right respectively. Where these are used for changes of direction then they imply a turn of about 90° when facing in the direction of the walk. 'Half L' and 'half R' indicate a half-turn, i.e. approximately 45°, and 'back half L' or 'back half R' indicate three quarter-turns, i.e. about 135°. PFS stands for 'Public Footpath Sign', PBS for 'Public Bridleway Sign' and OS for 'Ordnance Survey'.

7. ROUTE DESCRIPTION

9

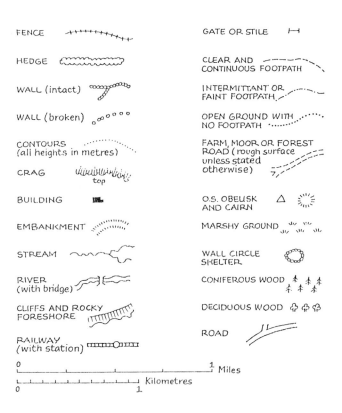

FENCE

GATE OR STILE

HEDGE

CLEAR AND CONTINUOUS FOOTPATH

WALL (intact)

INTERMITTANT OR FAINT FOOTPATH

WALL (broken)

OPEN GROUND WITH NO FOOTPATH

CONTOURS (all heights in metres)

FARM, MOOR OR FOREST ROAD (rough surface unless stated otherwise)

CRAG
top

BUILDING

O.S. OBELISK AND CAIRN

EMBANKMENT

MARSHY GROUND

STREAM

WALL CIRCLE SHELTER

RIVER (with bridge)

CONIFEROUS WOOD

CLIFFS AND ROCKY FORESHORE

DECIDUOUS WOOD

RAILWAY (with station)

ROAD

0   1 Miles

0   1 Kilometres

FIGURE 2 Symbols used on detailed route maps

To avoid constant repetition, it should be assumed that all stiles and gates mentioned in the route description are to be crossed (unless there is a specific statement otherwise).

8. STANDARD OF THE ROUTES

The briefest examination of the route descriptions that follow will show that the routes described cover an enormous range of both length and of difficulty; some of the easy routes at least can be undertaken by a family party, with care, at almost any time of the year while the hardest routes are only really suitable for experienced fell-walkers who are both fit and well-equipped. Any walker therefore who is contemplating following a route should make sure before starting that it is within their ability.

It is difficult in practice, however, to assess the difficulty of any route because it is dependent upon a number of factors and will in any case vary considerably from day to day with the weather. Any consideration of weather conditions must, of course, be left to the walker himself (but read the section on safety first). Apart from that, it is probably best to attempt an overall assessment of difficulty based upon the length, amount of ascent and descent, problems of route-finding and finally, upon the roughness of the terrain.

Each of the routes has therefore been given a grading based upon a consideration of these factors. A general description of each grade follows.

Easy (1): generally short walks (up to 5 miles, 8 km) over well-defined paths, with no problems of route-finding. Some climbing may be involved, but progress is mostly over fairly gradual slopes with only short sections of more difficult ground. The paths may, however, sometimes run alongside cliffs, streams or steep slopes where care should be taken — children must be kept in close control on certain sections of cliff-top path on the Pembrokeshire Coast Path.

Moderate (2): rather longer walks (up to about 10 miles, 16 km), mostly over paths, but with sections where route-finding will be more difficult. Mountain summits may be reached with climbing over steeper and rougher ground.

More strenuous (3): perhaps longer walks of over 10 miles, 16 km with prolonged spells of climbing. Some rough ground calling for good route-finding ability, perhaps with stretches of scrambling with some exposure.

The walks are arranged in order of increasing difficulty for each National Park, beginning with 1 (the easiest) in each case.

Finally, a summary of each walk is given at the head of each section with information on the distance, amount of climbing and any special difficulties, such as scrambling, that will be met along the way.

9. STARTING AND FINISHING POINTS

The majority of the routes are circular in order to avoid any problems with transport when the walk is completed.

The location of each starting and finishing point is given by the number of the appropriate Outdoor Leisure Landranger map with a six figure grid reference (see 'Giving a Grid Reference on page 124). The starting points are also shown on figure 1.

10. TIME FOR COMPLETION

The usual method of estimating the length of time needed for a walk is by Naismith's Rule: 'For ordinary walking allow one hour for every 3 miles (5 km) and add one hour for every 2000 feet (600 m) of ascent; for backpacking with a heavy load allow one hour for every $2\frac{1}{2}$ miles (4 km) and one hour for every 1500 feet (450 m) of ascent'. However, for many this tends to be over-optimistic and it is better for each walker to form an assessment of his own performance over one or two walks. Naismith's Rule also makes no allowance for rest or food stops or for the influence of weather conditions.

SELECTED WALKS IN THE SNOWDONIA NATIONAL PARK

*The old tramway from the South Snowdon Slate Quarry
crossed by the Watkin Path*

1·1

THROUGH THE LLUGWY GORGE

An extremely attractive walk along the Llugwy Gorge past the Ugly House, the Swallow Falls and the Miners' Bridge, including a stretch of the Gwydyr Forest. The Swallow Falls are probably the most popular tourist attraction in Wales, but almost everybody else will be on the opposite bank, where a charge is made for admission.

STARTING POINT
Ty-hyll (the Ugly House) (115-756575)
FINISHING POINT
Pont-y-Pair bridge, Betws-y-Coed (115-792567)
LENGTH
2¾ miles (4.5 km)
ASCENT
100 ft (30 m)

ROUTE DESCRIPTION (Map 1)

From the Ugly House (1), cross the minor road and pass the small private car-park to the end of the bridge (PFS). Go down the steps on to the river bank and walk downstream with the river to the R, soon crossing a stile into a wood. The path continues in the same direction, gradually rising above the river until the Swallow Falls (2) can be seen below. A superb path runs across the steep wooded hillside above the falls with rocks above and a steep fall down to the R towards the river. Despite this spectacular setting, however, there is no real danger as a guarding fence has been erected throughout.

Where the fence ends, reach open ground. The wide path to the L goes to the tea-gardens at Allt-isaf which can be used for a pleasant break. Otherwise, continue in the same direction along a narrow path crossing a small stream and through a plantation of young trees. After the plantation take the wide path which rises through mature trees to a forest track at the top (3). Here turn R to a road where turn R again. After about 50 yards (45 m) drop down to the R on to a lower and extremely pleasant path through the forest. The path is level to start with, but later descends steeply towards the river; carry on, crossing two small bridges near the river, until a splendid fenced viewpoint is reached overlooking rapids. Rise L up to the road.

Go R along the road for about 60 yards (55 m), then leave the road to the R dropping down by a fence to the Miners' Bridge (4). Do not cross, but continue downstream on the same side of the river, soon leaving the wood over a ladder stile. Continue

13

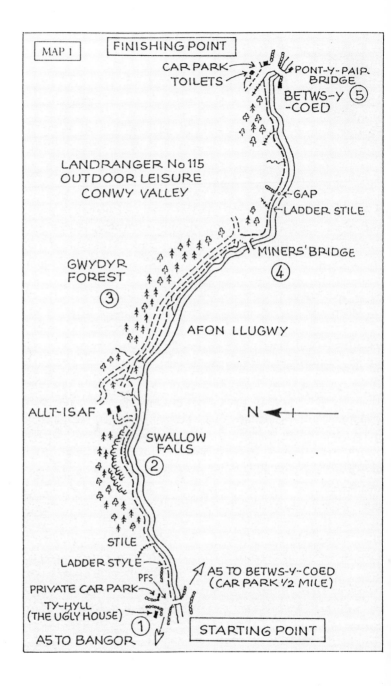

MAP 1

FINISHING POINT

CAR PARK →
TOILETS →
PONT-Y-PAIR. BRIDGE
BETWS-Y (5) -COED

LANDRANGER No 115
OUTDOOR LEISURE
CONWY VALLEY

← GAP
← LADDER STILE

MINERS' BRIDGE (4)

GWYDYR
FOREST
(3)

AFON LLUGWY

ALLT-ISAF

N ←┤────

SWALLOW
FALLS
(2)

STILE
LADDER STYLE →
PFS
PRIVATE CAR PARK →
TY-HYLL
(THE UGLY HOUSE) →
(1)
A5 TO BANGOR

A5 TO BETWS-Y-COED
(CAR PARK ½ MILE)

STARTING POINT

along the bank, over a small footbridge, then at the forest boundary over a ladder stile, later crossing a fence, until a road is reached opposite the car-park at the Pont-y-Pair bridge (5).

Opposite Afon Llugwy

1 *Ty-hyll, the Ugly House*
The Ugly House, which stands on the Capel Curig side of the

bridge over the Llugwy, lives up to its name. A rough and primitive building with slate roof and walls of unusual thickness, it was built about 1475. No mortar was used.

2 *The Swallow Falls*

A survey in 1975 showed that the Swallow Falls were visited by about 690,000 people annually. The majority of visitors approach the Falls from the road on the south side, where a car-park has been provided, paying a fee for the privilege. The Falls can also be viewed from the north bank, free of charge, using the public right-of-way; here the view is admittedly poorer but the walking much more exciting.

George Borrow, who visited North Wales in 1854 and wrote of his experiences in *Wild Wales*, which is now a classic still sold in local shops, described the Falls as follows: 'The Fall of the Swallow is not a majestic single fall, but a succession of small ones. First there are a number of little foaming torrents, bursting through rocks about twenty yards above the promontory, on which I stood. Then came two beautiful rolls of white water, dashing into a pool a little way above the promontory; then there is a swirl of water round its corner into a pool below on its right, black as death and seemingly of great depth; then a rush through a very narrow outlet into another pool, from which the water clamours away down the glen. Such is the Rhaiadr y Wennol, or Swallow Fall; called so from the rapidity with which the waters rush and skip along'.

3 *The Gwydyr Forest*

The walk passes through a lovely section of the forest, the property of the Forestry Commission. See page 48.

4 *The Miners' Bridge*

The Miners' Bridge over the Llugwy is inclined as a ladder from one bank to the other at an angle of about 30° to the horizontal. The bridge originally served as a convenient route for miners living nearby at Pentre-du, south of the river, to reach their work in the lead mines situated on the higher ground to the north. The present bridge was erected about 1983 and is the fifth or sixth on the site.

5 *Pont-y-Pair Bridge, Betws-y-Coed*

'The Bridge of the Cauldron', spanning the turbulent Llugwy by a series of five arches at the western end of Betws-y-Coed, is of uncertain date. It may be fifteenth century, built by a local man named Howel, but it may also be the work of Inigo Jones about 200 years later in the seventeenth. There are fine rapids upstream from the bridge — hence its name.

1·2

The Precipice Walk

A short and easy walk with little climbing around the two summits of Foel Cynwch and Foel Faner and the lovely Llyn Cynwch. For much of the route, the way is a narrow path running across the steep hillside high above the Afon Mawddach with superb views over the valley and the great forest of Coed y Brenin beyond.

This path is not a public right of way, but access has been granted by the Nannau Estate since 1890. The National Park Authority has provided stiles, waste bins and information boards around the walk. This should not be confused with the New Precipice Walk which is further to the west near Borthwnog.

ROUTE DESCRIPTION (Map 2)

Leave the car-park and turn L along the road past an Information Board. After a short distance turn L through a gate (sign 'Precipice Walk') and walk along a path between conifers.

STARTING AND FINISHING POINT Car-park at Saith groesffordd (124-746212). Leave Dolgellau on the A494 to Bala, branching L ¼ mile (400 m) after the bridge. Follow minor road for 2½ miles (4 km) through three junctions to reach car-park.
LENGTH
3½ miles (5.5 km)
ASCENT
125 ft (40 m)

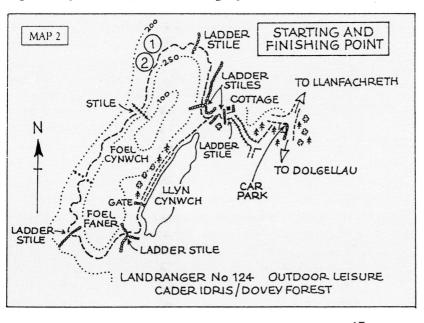

MAP 2

200
1 LADDER STILE
2 250
STARTING AND FINISHING POINT
LADDER STILES
TO LLANFACHRETH
COTTAGE
STILE
100
FOEL CYNWCH
LADDER STILE
TO DOLGELLAU
N
LLYN CYNWCH
CAR PARK
GATE
FOEL FANER
LADDER STILE
LADDER STILE
LANDRANGER No 124   OUTDOOR LEISURE CADER IDRIS / DOVEY FOREST

17

The path soon bends R and continues between fences to a cottage. Turn L before the cottage, up to a ladder stile. The path turns R after the stile and then bends to the L to reach a second ladder stile. Cross and shortly afterwards take the R fork at a path junction. The path climbs to a wall and bends R with it; continue with this wall keeping it to your R, crossing a further ladder stile.

The path from there is clear and follows the 800 ft (245 m) contour around Foel Cynwch and then further along around Foel Faner. Magnificent views open up as you progress along this walk, over the Mawddach Valley *(1)* and beyond to the Coed y Brenin Forest *(2)*. For a short distance the slope below the path is particularly steep, hence Precipice Walk.

Eventually the path bends away from the main valley crossing a ladder stile, and runs along the hillside to the L of a small dry valley. Cross another ladder stile and continue to the lake Llyn Cynwch, there cross a low wall and turn L. Walk along the L side of the lake to rejoin the original path at a junction. Return to the car-park.

1 The Gold Mines of the Mawddach

The gold belt of North Wales extended in an arc, about one mile wide along the valley of the Afon Mawddach from its estuary at Barmouth to its upper reaches within the Coed y Brenin Forest. Although some gold may have been extracted in this region prior to the nineteenth century, the industry really began in 1844 with the discovery of gold at the Cwmheisian Mines, which were being worked at that time for lead, and ended to all intents and purposes during World War I. A total of nearly 130,000 oz of gold was extracted during that period, of which the vast bulk came from two mines: the Clogau, between Barmouth and Dolgellau near the village of Bontddu, and Gwynfynydd, at the northern extremity of the field. Both mines were in continuous production from around 1890 to their closures in 1911 and 1916 respectively.

The gold occurs as very fine yellow particles embedded in veins of quartz, called lodes. The distribution of gold is by no means uniform, which accounts for the violent fluctuations in the output from the mines (and hence their profitability). A tunnel or level was driven along the lode until a gold-rich area was discovered, this would then be dug out, the extracted ore being taken up to the surface in small waggons. The ore was crushed to free the metallic particles, which were then separated from the waste by amalgamation with

Opposite *View towards The Precipice Walk*

mercury. The amount of waste was enormous; in the case of the Clogau, for instance, between 1900 and 1910 inclusive, its most successful years, no less than 108,329 tons of quartz had to be crushed to produce 54,970 oz of gold, a ratio of 52,972:1.

The wedding rings of Queen Elizabeth the Queen Mother (1923), The Queen (1947), The Princess Margaret (1960), The Princess Anne (1973) and The Princess of Wales (1981) were made from the same nugget of Welsh gold, which came from the Clogau. In 1981 the Royal British Legion presented the Queen with a sample of Welsh gold weighing 36g and it was from this that the wedding ring of the Duchess of York was made in 1986.

2 *Coed y Brenin Forest (The Forest of the King)*
Coed y Brenin Forest, owned by the Forest Authority and Forest Enterprise, covers an area of over 23,200 acres (9400 ha) round the valleys of the Afon Mawddach and its tributaries. Most of the land for the forest was purchased from the Vaughan family, owners of the local estate of Nannau — hence its original name of Vaughan Forest — and planting commenced in 1922. The name was changed to its present form in 1935 to commemorate the Silver Jubilee of George V. There are over 100 miles (160 km) of forest roads and paths open to walkers, of which approximately half have been waymarked, a nature trail, a mountain bothy, a small arboretum at Glasdir and a Visitor Centre near Maesgwm, 8 miles (13 km) north of Dolgellau on the A470.

1·3

TO THE RHAEADR-FAWR, THE ABER FALLS

A short but exceedingly pleasant walk which follows the river to the Rhaeadr-fawr, a spectacular waterfall 120 ft (37 m) high. Return by the same route or by a delightful path through a coniferous forest.

ROUTE DESCRIPTION (Map 3)

From the small car-park by the bridge over the Afon Aber go through the small gate to the L of the Park Information Board *(1)* (footpath sign to Aber Falls). Keep on the R side of the stream to a footbridge, cross and go through the gate on the far side into the farm road beyond. Turn R along the farm road and continue ahead, ignoring the farm road bending back to the L. Further along, bend round to the R of a small cottage. Soon after the cottage, where the farm road goes L and becomes faint, go ahead on a path through a gap in a wall and later through a gate. The falls are now directly ahead.

You can return, of course, by the same route but a much better way is to use a lovely woodland path which crosses the hillside to the R and which will give about the same distance. For this alternative path return to the gate, go through, then turn R over a ladder stile and climb away from the falls up the slope half L along the obvious path (the path is marked by short posts.

Eventually at the end of the rise go over a stile into a wood and follow the path ahead, keeping L at a path junction (do not follow the markers here, which are for the R-hand path). This delightful path through the forest is quite clear throughout. Eventually leave the wood over a stile and on through a wall gap to the R of a sheepfold. Continue in the same direction with a fence to your R to reach the farm road that you walked along earlier on your way to the falls. Turn R along it back to the car-park.

STARTING AND FINISHING POINT Bontnewydd (115-662720). From A55, turn up minor road in Aber by Aber Falls Hotel and Garage, and immediately R (sign on road). Continue up road for about ¼ mile (1.2 km) to small car-park by bridge over river; there is a further and larger car-park across the bridge.
LENGTH
3 miles (5 km)
ASCENT
500 ft (150 m)

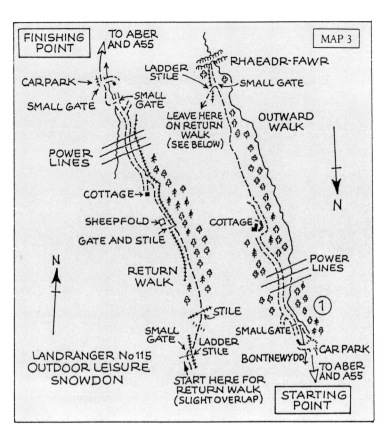

1 Coedydd Aber National Nature Reserve

The valley of the Afon Rhaeadr Fawr as far as the Aber Falls, the hilltop of Maes y Gaer and a small strip along the Afon Anafon together form the Reserve set up by the Nature Conservancy Council in 1975. Its main interest lies in its woodland of broad-leaved trees, mainly oak, a remnant of the great forests that once covered most of the valleys and the lower hillsides of North Wales.

The Aber Falls in winter   *Overleaf Bontnewydd. The starting point for Route 3*

1·4

THE ROMAN STEPS

An easy and clear path climbs slowly up from the lovely valley of Cwm Bychan, through a deciduous wood, to the famous Roman Steps, an ancient causeway of stone flags leading up the Bwlch Tyddiad. It is worth going on to the top of the col for the view to the east before returning by the same route. The route enters the Rhinog National Nature Reserve for a short distance.

ROUTE DESCRIPTION (Map 4)

Leave the car-park at Cwm Bychan and turn R along the road.

STARTING AND FINISHING POINT Cwm Bychan (124-646314). On the A496 from Barmouth to Harlech turn R at Llanbedr (signs to Cwm Bychan) and follow the very narrow and winding road to its end at the far side of the lake.
LENGTH
3 miles (5 km)
ASCENT
925 ft (280 m)

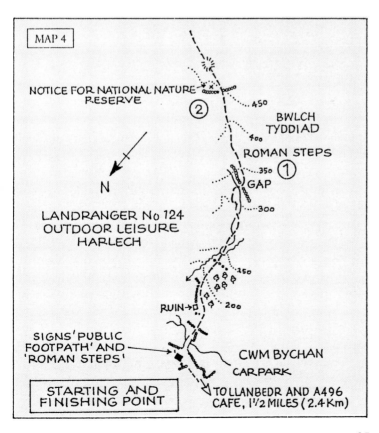

MAP 4

NOTICE FOR NATIONAL NATURE RESERVE
(2)
...450
BWLCH TYDDIAD
...400
ROMAN STEPS (1)
...350
GAP
...300
N
LANDRANGER No 124
OUTDOOR LEISURE
HARLECH
...250
RUIN→☐ 200
SIGNS 'PUBLIC FOOTPATH' AND 'ROMAN STEPS'
CWM BYCHAN
CAR PARK
STARTING AND FINISHING POINT
TO LLANBEDR AND A496
CAFE, 1½ MILES (2.4 Km)

25

The Roman Steps, Bwlch Tyddiad

Opposite a barn (on the L), turn R through a gate (signs 'Roman Steps' and 'Public Footpath'). The path crosses a stone causeway over a small stream and then continues, with a wall to the R, through a gap. Continue along this clear path, which slowly rises to pass to the R of a small ruin and through a deciduous wood. Beyond the wood the paths head towards a ravine, later swinging to the R to pass through a gap in a wall. Immediately after the gap the path turns L along a particularly fine section of the Roman Steps *(1)*.

Follow the Roman Steps, slowly climbing on the R-hand side of the ravine to eventually enter the Rhinog National Nature Reserve *(2)*. Continue in the same direction on the path as far as the large cairn at the top of the pass, from which there is a magnificent view.

Return by the same route back to Cwm Bychan.

1 The Roman Steps
The paved path running from Cwm Bychan to the Bwlch

Tyddiad is traditionally known as the Roman Steps, but its actual origin is obscure. Various theories place the path in the period of the Roman occupation, in Medieval times for the transport of wool from Bala to the sea at Llanbedr and Harlech, and as late as the seventeenth century as a local path for the occupiers of the farmstead at Cwm Bychan. This section of the path is in a fine state of preservation but other sections have been identified which are now neglected.

2 *Rhinog National Nature Reserve*
An area of 991 acres (401 ha) around the Bwlch Drws Ardudwy (The Pass of the Door of Ardudwy), which includes the summit of Rhinog Fawr. A difficult area for walking with thick heather and rock, and also one of the loneliest regions in the Park.

View of Lyn Cwn Bychan at the beginning of the Roman Steps walk

2·5
CONWY MOUNTAIN AND THE SYCHNANT PASS

STARTING POINT
Conwy Castle (115-784775)
FINISHING POINT
On the road from Conwy to the Sychnant Pass near Brynrhedyn (115-770775), about 1 mile (1.6 km) from Conwy.
LENGTH
6½ miles (10.5 km)
ASCENT
1475 ft (450 m)

The northern tip of the Snowdonia National Park contains two scenic gems: Conwy Mountain (Mynydd y Dref), which gives magnificent views over Conwy and the north coast of Wales, and the Sychnant Pass, which carried the old road over the high ground to the west of Conwy. This walk from Conwy links them both with a pleasant stretch up the wooded valley of the Afon Gyrach.

ROUTE DESCRIPTION (Maps 5, 6)

From Castle Square in Conwy *(1) (2)*, walk down Rose Hill Street, soon bending R with it to pass through Lancaster Square and the gateway in the town wall directly ahead. Continue along the Bangor Road (A55) from the gateway, taking the second road to the L (sign 'Conwy Mountain and Sychnant Pass'). Immediately after crossing the railway bridge, turn R and walk along Cadnant Park Road following it past the cul-de-sac of Cadnant Park. After the cul-de-sac and a L bend, take the first road to the R (Mountain Road). At the end of the road at a junction, bend L (sign 'To Mountain Road') and follow the rough road up to a fork in front of some cottages (Machno Cottages). Take the R fork and pass in front of the cottages to continue along a narrow path through bushes. The path climbs steadily to the R through bracken up towards the ridge top. There are many paths around the mountain: follow the one that keeps on or close to the ridge top for magnificent views on three sides. Eventually reach the cairns on top of Conwy Mountain *(3)*.

Continue over the top to pick up a broad track; this bends down on the R of the ridge and then goes over the ridge to the L to descend to a wall. Turn R and follow the wall to its end (i.e. where it bends L) near a small pool and the junction of three paths. Take the path to the L to a fence and a cross-path. Continue along the track across heading in the same direction and descending to a farm road, there turn R and go around the head of a spectacular valley (by the Sychnant Pass) *(4)*. Do not

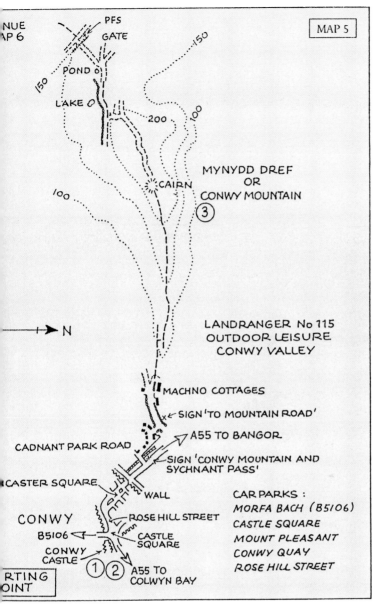

MAP 5

NUE
\P 6
PFS
GATE
150
POND ᵒ
150
LAKE ᴏ
200
100
CAIRN
100
MYNYDD DREF
OR
CONWY MOUNTAIN
③

→ N

LANDRANGER No 115
OUTDOOR LEISURE
CONWY VALLEY

MACHNO COTTAGES
←SIGN 'TO MOUNTAIN ROAD'
↗A55 TO BANGOR
CADNANT PARK ROAD
←SIGN 'CONWY MOUNTAIN AND
SYCHNANT PASS'
ICASTER SQUARE
WALL
CONWY
ROSE HILL STREET
B5106
CASTLE
SQUARE
CONWY
CASTLE
①② A55 TO
COLWYN BAY
RTING
OINT

CAR PARKS :
MORFA BACH (B5106)
CASTLE SQUARE
MOUNT PLEASANT
CONWY QUAY
ROSE HILL STREET

continue as far as the road ahead, but drop down some steps at the head of the valley to the R and follow a path through the valley to reach a road by some cottages. Turn L and then R at a road junction to descend to Capelulo (café and hotels).

Turn L up the minor road immediately after the Fairy Glen Hotel and follow it as far as a bridge over a stream to the L. Cross and follow the drive to a house, here turn back half L along a path which then bends R and climbs the hillside (look back as you climb for lovely views over Capelulo towards the sea). At the top, go to the L of a wall and follow it past a farmhouse. Go over the top into a small valley; just before a

29

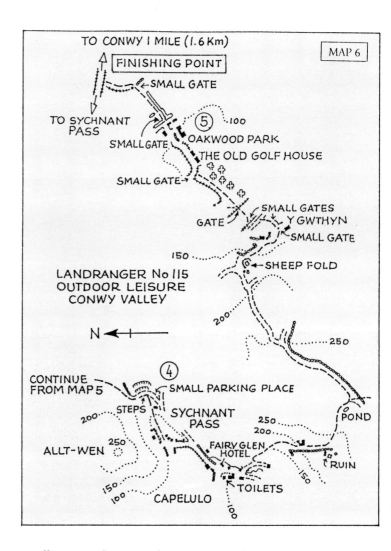

small group of trees and a ruin (over the wall to the R) turn L down a shallow valley to reach a crossing wall. Turn L and follow the wall until it bends R; just beyond the bend, go L at a path junction and to the L of a prominent hill to a T-junction by some sheepfolds. Here turn R and follow the path to a road. Turn R in the road and then L through a small gate just before the next house (Y Bwthyn).

Go past the house garage to a second small gate and then, with a fence on your R, to a third small gate. Here, go half L across a field to still another small gate and on again through a large gate; later reach a lane at the L edge of a wood by a cottage. Turn R and follow the lane to pass an exceptionally

Opposite Sychnant Pass and Conwy Mountain

large house on the R *(5)* and then on to meet a minor road. Turn R and then almost immediately L through a gate. Follow the hedge on your R to its end (i.e. where it swings R), then keep in the same direction to a small gate. Immediately after the gate turn L and go to road (PFS). Turn R and follow the road for about 1 mile (1.6 km) back to Conwy.

1 *Conwy Castle*

A Cistercian monastery holding the Charter of Llewelyn the Great and built on the site of the present parish church marked the beginning of the modern town of Conwy. But much more significant was the construction in the remarkably short time of four years between 1283 and 1287 of a great castle and fortified town on the orders of Edward I, to safeguard his recent victories over the Welsh. Since then the castle has played a part in other struggles: the rising of Owain Glyndŵr, the Wars of the Roses and the Civil War. During the summer arrange your return to Conwy after dusk, when the walls are floodlit to produce a superb spectacle.

2 *Telford's Suspension Bridge and Stephenson's Tubular Bridge*

Two famous bridges span the Conwy: the Suspension Bridge built by Thomas Telford in 1822 to carry a road and the Tubular Bridge constructed by George Stephenson in 1846–48 for the railway track. The latter is still in use, but the former was superseded by a modern bridge and is now owned by the National Trust.

3 *Castell Caer Lleion*

The summit of Conwy Mountain was the site of the Celtic hill-fort of Castell Caer Lleion probably built in the early Iron Age. The site was well chosen on a promontory with hillsides falling away steeply on all sides and high cliffs to the north, its isolated position giving it a magnificent view over the surrounding countryside. The fort occupied about 10 acres (4 ha) and was further strengthened by the building of ramparts, which are still visible.

4 *The Sychnant Pass*

The Sychnant Pass (the name means 'Dry Gorge') carried the old road from Conwy to the west thus avoiding the difficulty of forcing a road past the headland of Penmaen-bach. The road was used for this purpose until 1826.

5 *Oakwood Park*

This unusual house with square tower and spire was originally a private house, but in its time has also served as a hotel, war-time school and hospital for mentally handicapped children.

Opposite *Landscape near Dwygyfylchi*

2·6

THE PONY TRACK TO PENYGADAIR (NORTHERN ROUTE)

STARTING AND
FINISHING POINT
Ty-nant car-park
(124-698153).
Leave Dolgellau
along the A493
towards the toll
bridge and Tywyn.
Fork L on minor
road. The car-park
is on R after 2½
miles (4 km). There
is a small
information point
nearby which is
open in summer.
LENGTH
5 miles (8 km)
ASCENT
2400 ft (730 m)

A short and straightforward route to the summit of Cader Idris, except for the final ascent where the path rises more steeply over rougher ground along the edge of a deep and impressive cwm with a considerable drop to the left. The track has been extensively repaired and well-marked with signs and cairns throughout, and no difficulty will be found in following it. The views, particularly from the final summit ridge, are magnificent. Return by the same route.

ROUTE DESCRIPTION (Map 7)

Walk from the car-park into the road and turn R. At a telephone box (PFS) turn L over a stile and go up the farm road beyond soon passing a farm. After the farm, continue ahead through a gate, over a small bridge and uphill with a stream and wood on the L. At a footpath sign turn R, leaving the farm road through a gap, and go between two walls, soon bending L to a small gate. After the gate the path bends R over a small stream and then L uphill through a gap to a small gate in a wall. Continue up the hill moving R to a further wall with a small gate. Go through the gate and follow a path with a wall on the R.

Where the wall bends away, the path rises steeply up the ridge ahead through zig-zags, eventually passing through a gap (Rhiw Gwredydd). The path goes half L keeping near to the fence on the L. Where the fence turns to the L continue ahead up steps following a line of cairns. The path goes up the mountainside gradually approaching the lip of a great cliff dropping L into the depths of an impressive cwm, with Llyn y Gadair far below. Continue along the path on the edge of the cliff rising steeply to the summit of Penygadair. Return by the same route back to Ty-nant.

Opposite Cader Idris

34

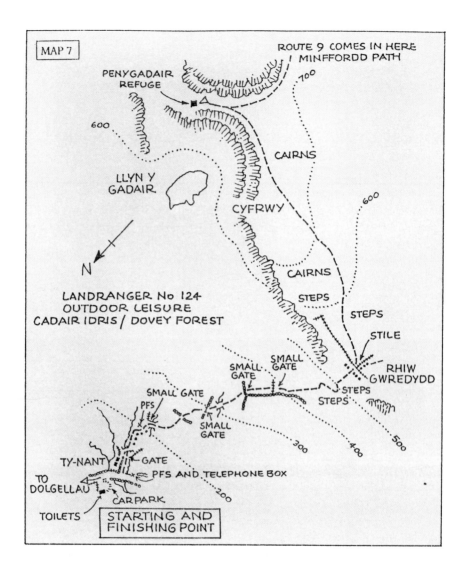

2·7

THE ASCENT OF MOEL HEBOG

Moel Hebog, the Bald Hill of the Hawk, is one of the best-known mountains in North Wales. Its ascent from Beddgelert is steep and involves some light scrambling up broken slopes of scree and rock, but the effort is well worthwhile for the top is a magnificent viewpoint. You can return by the same route, but a much better alternative is to descend down grassy slopes to the north-west to visit the cave of Owain Glyndŵr before returning by a long and interesting forest path back to Beddgelert.

STARTING AND
FINISHING POINT
Beddgelert (115-589481)
LENGTH
5½ miles (9 km)
ASCENT
2350 ft (720 m)

ROUTE DESCRIPTION (Map 8)

Go up the small road to the R of the Royal Goat Hotel. Immediately after the hotel, turn R and go through a gate (do not turn L by the gate as indicated by the PFS), and continue to reach the old track of the Welsh Highland Railway *(1)*. Just past a small concrete tower turn L through a gate into a narrow sunken lane. Turn R along the lane and follow it as it bends L by a stream and on to a gate. Beyond, cross a bridge and turn L in a further lane. Follow this lane to the farm of Cwm Cloch.

Immediately after the barn on the R, turn R, cross a ladder stile and follow a footpath up the hill ('Walking Man' signs) to a further ladder stile by a sheepfold. Keep climbing the hill to a gap in a wall (there are cairns on both sides of the gap) and up again to a small gate in the mountain wall. Above this wall the path rises steadily, later becoming steeper and climbing over broken rocks and scree (it is clearly marked throughout with cairns). Much later, reach the ridge top by two large cairns; turn L and climb the final ridge to the summit of Moel Hebog.

For your return, go past the OS obelisk and continue downhill to the R of the summit wall (do not cross the ladder stile nearby). This leads down easy slopes to a col, Bwlch Meillionen *(2)*. Just after some small bends in the wall, take a faint path half R to leave the descent wall and go to a second wall running across (i.e. by cutting the corner). Turn R and follow the path down. Go through a gap and continue down to the forest below

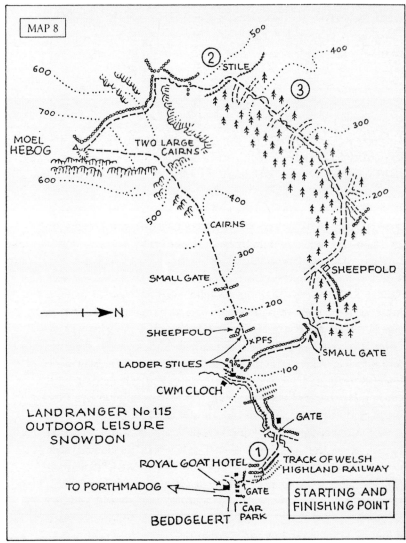

MAP 8

500
400
② STILE
③
600
700
300
MOEL
HEBOG
TWO LARGE
CAIRNS
600
400
500
CAIRNS
300
200
SMALL GATE
→ N
200
SHEEPFOLD → XPFS
LADDER STILES
100
CWM CLOCH

SHEEPFOLD
SMALL GATE

LANDRANGER No 115
OUTDOOR LEISURE
SNOWDON

GATE

ROYAL GOAT HOTEL ① TRACK OF WELSH
HIGHLAND RAILWAY

TO PORTHMADOG ←
GATE
CAR
PARK
BEDDGELERT

STARTING AND
FINISHING POINT

38

(3). Turn L along the forest fence to reach a stile.

Cross into the forest and follow a path downhill across six forest roads. The path meets a small stream between the first and second forest roads and thereafter drops with it; the path is also marked throughout with red waymarks. At the sixth forest road turn R. (If you lose count of forest roads during the long descent, remember that there is a stone wall soon after the sixth and final forest road. If you do meet this, then retrace your steps back a few yards.)

Continue down to a junction. Take the L junction and immediately leave to the L down a footpath (to the R of a sheepfold). Continue down through the forest to a further forest road. Here turn R and follow it until it bends R; at this bend take a path to the L which crosses a stream and goes to a gate. Beyond, continue to the L of a wall, eventually crossing it through the second gate on the R. Continue across the field to a ladder stile by a barn. You are now back to Cwm Cloch and your way back to Beddgelert is down the lane to the L.

Approaching Cwm Cloch

1 *The Welsh Highland Railway*
The route crosses the site of the Beddgelert station on the Welsh Highland Railway. The construction of the line between Caernarfon and Rhyd-ddu was completed in 1881, but the prosperity of the line declined after the opening of the Snowdon Mountain Railway in 1896. The line was revived in the early 1920s when the final section of the railway to Porthmadog was built. This operated for fourteen years.

The Welsh Highland Railway Society was formed in 1961 with the intention of opening as much of the original line as possible and operating it with steam traction. The society became The Welsh Highland Light Railway (1964) Ltd. three years later.

2 *Ogof Owain Glyndŵr*
The peak of Moel yr Ogof has a number of horizontal clefts on its eastern face. The largest of these is said to be the hiding place of Owain Glyndŵr (Owen Glendower) when pursued by the English.

Wales had remained an independent kingdom until the middle thirteenth century despite numerous attempts to subdue it. In several years (1282–84) of ruthless warfare, however, Edward 1 overran Wales and built a series of powerful castles at Conwy, Harlech and elsewhere to safeguard his conquests. Despite serious revolts in 1287 and 1294 the Welsh generally accepted the rule of the English and were gradually absorbed both into the administration of Wales and into the English armies in their wars against France and Scotland. In 1400, however, a more serious revolt began under Owain Glyndŵr, a man raised as an English gentleman, but who had from his ancestry the strongest claim for the title of Prince of Wales. Within a few years the revolt had spread throughout Wales, the great castles of Aberystwyth and Harlech had fallen and an independent government had been formed supported by an alliance with the French.

By 1410, however, the tide had turned, the castles had been re-taken and Owain Glyndŵr had become a hunted fugitive. We hear of him in 1415 and then no more.

The cave can be reached from the top of the forest.

3 *The Beddgelert Forest*
Beddgelert Forest is part of the Snowdonia National Forest Park. There is a Forestry Commission campsite within the Forest, a wayfaring course and several forest walks.

The view towards Moel Hebog

2·8

THE ASCENT OF MOEL SIABOD

STARTING AND
FINISHING POINT
Plas y Brenin, near
Capel Curig (115-
716578). Plas y
Brenin is the very
large building on
the L about 550 yd
(500 m) from Capel
Curig along the
road (A4086) to
Llanberis and
Beddgelert.
LENGTH
6½ miles (10.5 km)
ASCENT
2225 ft (680 m)

From Plas y Brenin, forest roads and paths run through beautiful woods by the Afon Llugwy to reach the old bridge of Pont Cyfyng. From there, a long gradual climb leads up the eastern flank of Moel Siabod to reach the ridge of Daiar Ddu above Llyn y Foel. The Daiar Ddu gives a long but easy scramble, finishing at the summit cairn. The summit ridge is traversed, followed by a descent over grassy slopes to the coniferous forests above Plas y Brenin. The view from the footbridge at Plas y Brenin towards the Snowdon Horseshoe is considered one of the finest in Snowdonia.

ROUTE DESCRIPTION (Maps 9, 10)

Go through a small gate (PFS) to the R of the main building of Plas y Brenin (1) and descend to a footbridge. Immediately after the footbridge, turn L along a forest road which runs along the R-hand side of a small lake. Keep along this forest road passing a house on the L and another forest road coming in from the R. Take a second forest road to the R just afterwards and follow it to its end at some steps, where a path continues in the same direction. Follow this path to a footbridge. Do not cross, but instead turn R and keep along the R bank of the river passing over a ladder stile and then through a gate. Beyond go to the L of a small barn, then head slightly R for a gap in a fence at the front of a farmhouse. Go through the gap, over a small stream and up to the house wall, there turn L. Rise to a gate which leads into a minor road and turn R.

Follow the road, turning R at a junction after 100 yards (90 m), until it ends at the farm of Rhôs; there continue on the rough road beyond to a ladder stile by an old house and then on again to a second ladder stile in a fence (2). Higher still, take the L fork at a junction and, crossing a third ladder stile, continue to a lake. Follow the clear path to the R of the lake and then up to some slate quarries ahead (3). Go past the spoil heaps and ruined buildings of the quarry and on to the L of a deep sinister

Opposite The Snowdon Horseshoe from the Llynnau Mymbyr

42

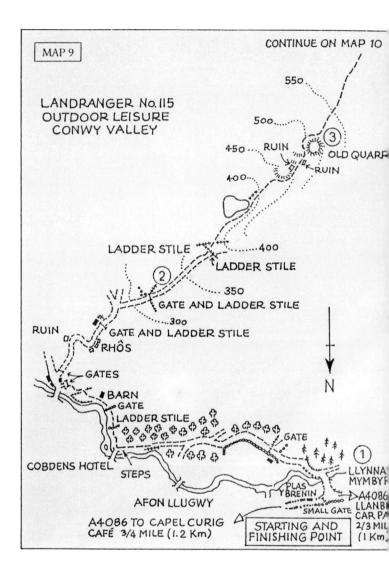

MAP 9

CONTINUE ON MAP 10

550

LANDRANGER No.115
OUTDOOR LEISURE
CONWY VALLEY

500

450 · RUIN

③

OLD QUARF

RUIN

400

LADDER STILE · · · · · · 400

LADDER STILE

②

350

GATE AND LADDER STILE

300

RUIN

GATE AND LADDER STILE

RHÔS

GATES

BARN
GATE
LADDER STILE

GATE

①

N

COBDENS HOTEL
STEPS

LLYNNA
MYMBYF

PLAS
Y BRENIN

A4086

LLANBI
CAR PA

AFON LLUGWY

SMALL GATE

A4086 TO CAPEL CURIG
CAFÉ 3/4 MILE (1.2 Km)

STARTING AND
FINISHING POINT

2/3 MIL
(1 Km.

pit filled with black water into which the water cascades on the far side. The path continues beyond the pit up the valley to reach the top of a ridge from which a second lake can be seen. Keep on the path to pass this lake also on its R side and continue on to a further ridge ahead (there is a splendid view from here of the Lledr Valley) (4). Turn R and climb up the ridge following a path and cairns to the OS obelisk on the summit.

For the return, turn R from your approach route along the rocky summit ridge to the far end and drop down to the start of the grassy slopes of the mountain, here turn half L leading downhill (aim for the R-hand end of the lake in the valley). There is no path at first, but later you should be able to pick up

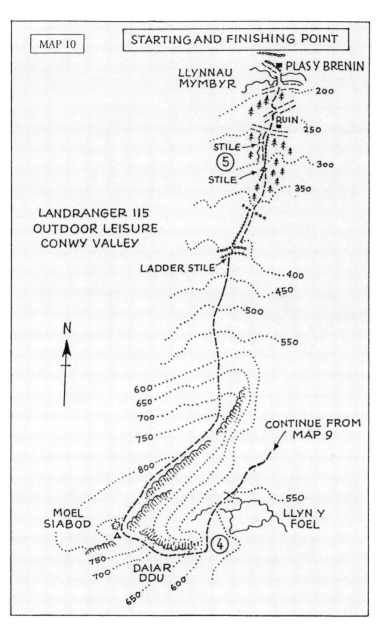

MAP 10

STARTING AND FINISHING POINT

PLAS Y BRENIN

LLYNNAU MYMBYR

200

RUIN

250

STILE

(5)

300

STILE

350

LANDRANGER 115
OUTDOOR LEISURE
CONWY VALLEY

LADDER STILE

400

450

500

550

N

600
650
700
750

800

CONTINUE FROM
MAP 9

550

MOEL
SIABOD

LLYN Y
FOEL

(4)

750
700

DAIAR
DDU

600

650

a path; follow it down to a ladder stile in a fence. Cross and
continue to descend on a rough path, with a fence on the L, to a
forest (5). Continue to follow the path down through the forest
to a stile in a fence and then later to meet a forest road. Cross
half R to go on a path to the L of a small ruined hut, and then
down a particularly delightful stretch of path under trees. At a
crossing track turn R, then immediately L and down again to
reach the bridge by Plas y Brenin.

45

THE ASCENT OF MOEL SIABOD

1 *Plas y Brenin (The King's House)*

The Old Road up the Nant Ffrancon Pass was constructed by
Richard Pennant – owner of the great quarry at Bethesda – to
connect his lands at Bethesda and near Bangor with those at
Capel Curig. At the latter place he built an inn, the Capel
Curig Inn, in 1800–1801 to serve the tourist trade. In later
years, 1808–1848, it also served the Royal Mail Coach which
carried the Irish Mail up the new turnpike between Shrews-
bury and Holyhead. George Borrow, author of *Wild Wales*,
visited the inn in 1854 on a day's walk from Cerrig-y-
Drudion to Bangor and found it '... a very magnificent
edifice ... from whose garden Snowdon may be seen
towering in majesty at the distance of about six miles'. Other
visitors over the years included Queen Victoria, Edward VIII,
Sir Walter Scott, Queen Mary, George V and Lord Byron. In
1870–71 – no doubt as a result of this heavy visitation by
royalty – the name of the inn was changed to the Royal
Hotel.

During World War II, the inn was taken over as a training
centre for mountain warfare, but returned to its former use
afterwards. In 1954, however, it was purchased by the
Central Council for Physical Recreation and opened in 1955
as The Snowdonia National Recreation Centre. In a reorgani-
zation during the early 1970s the CCPR was replaced by the
Sports Council, who became responsible for the management
of the Centre. It is now called Plas y Brenin, The National
Centre for Mountain Activities.

2 *Bryn-y-Gefeiliau*

The conquest of the Ordovices in Snowdonia in AD 78 by the
Roman Army under Agricola marked the end of active
campaigning in Wales; their control over a vanquished foe
was then assured by a series of forts placed at strategic points
and joined together by roads, along which supplies and
reinforcements could be speedily passed. One such fort was
built about 1½ miles (2.4 km) from Capel Curig towards
Betws-y-Coed, where the great Roman road of Sarn Helen
from Carmarthen to the Conwy Valley crossed the River
Llugwy. It was built early in the second century and formed a
permanent base for an auxiliary unit of perhaps 500 or 1000
men. The site can be seen from about the second ladder stile
on the climb up to Moel Siabod, it is to the R of the camp site
(brightly coloured tents) in the valley behind you.

3 *The Capel Curig Slate Quarry Company*

The deep and awesome pit, by the path to Moel Siabod was

*Opposite View from
the footbridge behind
Plas y Brenin*

Looking towards Moel Siabod from the road into Capel Curig

worked by the Capel Curig Slate Quarry Company from the nineteenth century. The company was amalgamated with several others in 1918 to form the Caernarvonshire Crown Slate Quarries Company but, like most other slate quarries in the area, closed down later.

4 *Dolwyddelan Castle*

From the bottom of the ridge beyond Llyn y Foel and before the final climb to the summit of Moel Siabod there is a splendid view of the Lledr valley ahead and half left. The prominent castle, perched on the edge of a rocky crag which falls steeply into the valley below, is Dolwyddelan. Built by a Prince of Gwynedd in the thirteenth century, it was reconstructed later in the same century by Edward I as part of his massive programme of castle building. The present remains consist of the rectangular keep to the east, the smaller West Tower, ditches and part of the curtain-wall.

5 *The Gwydyr Forest*

The forest behind Plas y Brenin is part of the Gwydyr Forest acquired by the Forestry Commission in 1920. The plantings have been of conifers, but there is a belt of natural oak to the north of the forest towards Capel Curig.

2·9

THE TRAVERSE OF CADER IDRIS

Cader Idris is one of the most popular mountains in Snowdonia, most people climbing it by the Pony Track from the Dolgellau side. The Minffordd Path from the south, however, is far better, reaching the summit by a long ridge that gives grand views to the left over the Tal-y-llyn Valley and to the right down high cliffs into the magnificent Cwm Cau. Even better than that is a traverse of the mountain, using both routes with a diversion to the summit of Cyfrwy.

STARTING POINT
Snowdonia National Park car-park and picnic site. The entrance is at the junction of B4405 with A487.
FINISHING POINT
Car-park at Ty-nant (124-698153)
LENGTH
6 miles (9.5 km)
ASCENT
2900 ft (880 m)

ROUTE DESCRIPTION (Maps 11, 7 — see also page 36)

(1) Leave the car-park by the kissing gate near the toilet block. Walk up an old drive under trees to an old house — Ystradlyn. Pass through another kissing gate. Continue in front of the house and enter the Cader Idris National Nature Reserve *(2)* through a small gate in the boundary fence. Then follow a path which rises steeply up through a wood; here, a river to the R of the path falls in a magnificent series of white cascades. At a small stream coming across to join the main stream, the path bends L and then R over the stream to resume the same direction as before. Pass through a small gate in a wall and continue rising along a path leaving the wood behind. The path goes up the hillside, at first with the stream still to the R, but later swinging L gradually leaving it. Go past two Reserve enclosures and on up the valley towards the small ridge ahead.

Eventually, reach a large cairn where the path forks. Take the L-hand path which rises steeply uphill (cairns) to reach the crest of a higher ridge. As you climb, Llyn Cau becomes visible down to the R. Continue to follow the path that goes up the ridge to the R, well-marked with cairns, with good views on both sides. Later reach a fence at the summit of Craig Cau, and continue across the top to drop down to Bwlch Cau. There is a considerable cliff to the R throughout this section and care is necessary, particularly in windy conditions, if you keep near to the edge for the excellent views. From Bwlch Cau, ascend on a

49

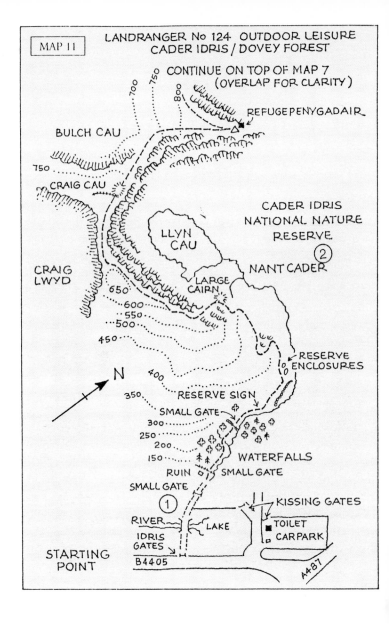

MAP 11

LANDRANGER No 124 OUTDOOR LEISURE
CADER IDRIS / DOVEY FOREST

CONTINUE ON TOP OF MAP 7
(OVERLAP FOR CLARITY)

REFUGE PENYGADAIR

BULCH CAU

CRAIG CAU

CADER IDRIS
NATIONAL NATURE
RESERVE
②

NANT CADER

LLYN
CAU

CRAIG
LWYD

LARGE
CAIRN

650
600
550
500
450

N

400

350

RESERVE SIGN

SMALL GATE
300
250
200
150

RESERVE
ENCLOSURES

WATERFALLS

RUIN
SMALL GATE

SMALL GATE

①

RIVER
IDRIS
GATES
B4405

LAKE

KISSING GATES

TOILET
CAR PARK

A487

STARTING
POINT

path following cairns to the os obelisk on the summit.

From the summit, looking back on your approach route, descend slightly R of your approach route on a path with a crag to the R. The path keeps near to the cliff edge for some way, then swings L and away from the edge; where the path swings away leave the path and climb keeping to the L of the cliff edge to the summit of Cyfrwy. Leave the summit SW to pick up the path again lower down the mountainside. The path descends steadily to meet a fence (on your R) and then on to a wall corner.

Here, cross to the R by a gate and then pass through a gap in a broken wall beyond to continue the descent. Go down zig-zags

Opposite Cader Idris seen from across Afon Mawddach

50

and down on a clear path to a wall, there turn R and follow the wall to a small gate. After the gate, the path bends L, goes through a gate and then a wall gap. Lower down still it swings R to a further small gate. Go through this gate and along a path between two walls into a lane, there turn L. Follow the lane over a bridge and through gates to reach a road. Turn R and walk the short distance to a car-park (if some kind person is waiting for you) or continue about 3 miles (5 km) to Dolgellau (if not).

1 *The Bala Fault and the Tal-y-llyn Valley*
The straight line and the steep sides of the Tal-y-llyn Valley make it one of the most impressive sights in North Wales. It is the result of a combination of forces: movements in the earth's crust, river erosion and glacial action.

Movements in the earth's crust can produce enormous forces of compression and tension which may, over long periods of time, result in extensive folding of the surface layers. In some cases the forces involved are so great that faults are formed — miles in length and thousands of feet deep — along which an immense thrusting action occurs with a relative displacement of the rocks on the opposite sides.

The valleys from Bala to Tywyn mark the line of such a fault, usually called the Bala Fault. In this case, the rocks on the south side have been displaced about 2 miles (3.2 km) from those on the north side. The rock along the fault line was mudstone, a soft, weak and easily eroded rock, which would have been extensively shattered during the progress of the faulting. This line of soft and shattered rock was rapidly worn away by river action to produce a deep and steep-sided valley. Finally, the river valley itself was deepened and straightened further by glacial action during the Ice Age; the lake of Tal-y-llyn probably forming later in a hollow in the valley gouged out by the ice. An excellent view of the valley is obtained as you come south-west down the A487 from the Cross Foxes Inn.

2 *Cader Idris National Nature Reserve*
A substantial part of Cader Idris from the Tal-y-llyn Valley to the summit ridge between Penygadair and Mynydd Moel, including Llyn Cau, has been designated as a National Nature Reserve. The main attractions are the oak woodland, typical of the forests that once covered most of the valleys and low hillsides of Wales, and the superb Cwm Cau, which shows the usual characteristics of glaciation.

Opposite Approach *to Cader Idris from Minffordd Path*

52

2·10

THE TRAVERSE OF SNOWDON

STARTING POINT
Bethania (115-627506) on the
A498 3 miles
(5 km) from
Beddgelert.
FINISHING POINT
Pen-y-Pass (115-647557)
LENGTH
10 miles (16 km)
ASCENT
2400 ft (730 m)

The Horseshoe is by far the most difficult of the usual routes up Snowdon, but the Miners' Track and the Watkin Path have the greatest interest. This route uses the Watkin Path for the ascent and the Miners' Track for the descent. Both paths are well-marked throughout and for most of their length give no difficulty in walking. The difficult sections are the final rise of the Watkin Path over steep scree to the summit of Yr Wyddfa, and the descent down the Miners' Track as far as Glaslyn.

ROUTE DESCRIPTION (Maps 12 — 14)

Leave the car-park at Bethania into the main road and turn L. Walk along the road, soon turning R down a small lane over a cattle grid (sign 'Public Footpath to Snowdon'). This is the start of the Watkin Path *(1)*. Continue up the lane soon leaving the tarmac road to the L up a rough road (sign 'Llwybr Watkin Path'). Further along, pass through a gate and continue to follow the old mine road, soon with open ground on both sides. The path swings R then L, with a river below on the R. As you climb, there is a good view of waterfalls ahead and the track passes over the old tramway from the South Snowdon Slate Quarry. Beyond, go through a gate to enter the Yr Wyddfa-Snowdon National Nature Reserve *(2) (3)*.

The path continues to the L of the stream, but crosses a bridge to the R bank just before the ruin at Plas Cwm Llan *(4)*. Pass the ruin and the Gladstone Rock *(5)* further along and proceed to the miners' barracks and quarries. At the barracks, the path swings R keeping to the R of a large waste heap. The path from here is rougher and rises more steeply, but is very clear and in any case is well-marked with cairns and the occasional sign. Continue up the mountainside to reach a large cairn on a col with a path coming in from the R (this is the path from Y Lliwedd); here go L and cross the col. On the far side of the col, the path rises very steeply, slanting L up a great shattered face of scree and rock. Reach the ridge at the top

54

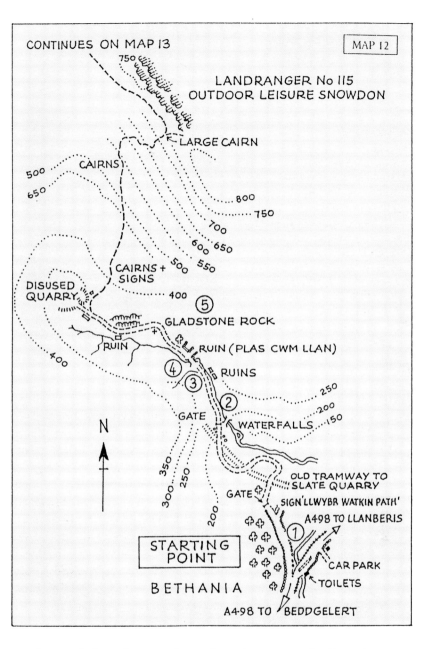

MAP 12

750

LANDRANGER No 115
OUTDOOR LEISURE SNOWDON

LARGE CAIRN

CAIRNS

500
650

800

750

700

600 650

500 550

CAIRNS +
SIGNS

DISUSED
QUARRY

400

⑤

GLADSTONE ROCK

RUIN

RUIN (PLAS CWM LLAN)

400

④

③

RUINS

②

GATE

WATERFALLS

250

200

150

N

350
300 250

200

OLD TRAMWAY TO
SLATE QUARRY

GATE

SIGN 'LLWYBR WATKIN PATH'

A498 TO LLANBERIS

①

STARTING
POINT

CAR PARK

TOILETS

BETHANIA

A498 TO BEDDGELERT

(rock monolith) and turn R for a short distance to the Summit
Hotel *(6) (7) (8)*.

Leave the Summit Hotel at the far end (i.e. from the station)
and descend on the path by the railway track to reach a rock
monolith on Bwlch Glas. (Note: there is a second monolith
lower down where the Snowdon Ranger Path meets the railway
line.) Here drop to the R from the ridge down zig-zags at the
top of the Miners' Track. Descend the Miners' Track until a
junction of paths is reached above a lake (Glaslyn), here
descend steeply to the R to reach the lake by the ruins of some

55

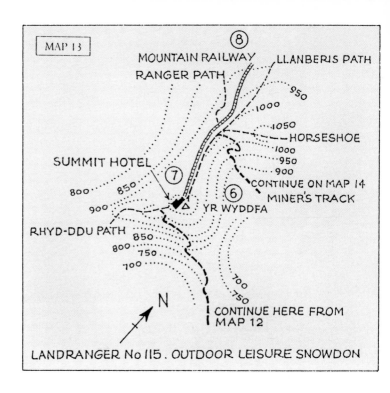

MAP 13

⑧
MOUNTAIN RAILWAY   LLANBERIS PATH
RANGER PATH

950
1000
1050
HORSESHOE
1000
950
900
CONTINUE ON MAP 14
MINER'S TRACK

SUMMIT HOTEL
⑦
800   850
900
YR WYDDFA ⑥

RHYD-DDU PATH
850
800
750
700

700
750

N

CONTINUE HERE FROM
MAP 12

LANDRANGER No 115. OUTDOOR LEISURE SNOWDON

old miners' barracks (9). (Do not go too far to the R, where there are dangerous mines.) Turn L to follow the broad path around the L shore of the lake and continue on, eventually reaching a lower and larger lake, Llyn Llydaw. Keep on the L shore of this lake past old mine buildings *(9) (10)*, later, to cross a causeway *(11)*. Follow the clear path beyond the lake *(12)* and down by a third and lower lake, Llyn Teyrn, to eventually reach Pen-y-Pass *(13)*.

1 *The Watkin Path*

This path was constructed by Sir Edward Watkin who, in the late eighteenth century, acquired an area of land near Bethania in the valley of Nant Gwynant; his house, called The Chalet, was built in the woods there. The path was intended to connect his house with the summit of Snowdon and was opened by the then Prime Minister, W. E. Gladstone, in 1892 (see page 60). Sir Edward, a rich and influential railway owner, should also be remembered for his attempt to construct a tunnel under the English Channel, before he was stopped by the Government of the day.

2 *Yr Wyddfa-Snowdon National Nature Reserve*

4145 acres (1678 hectares) of Snowdon were established as a National Nature Reserve by the Nature Conservancy Council

Opposite Y Lliwedd from Yr Wyddfa

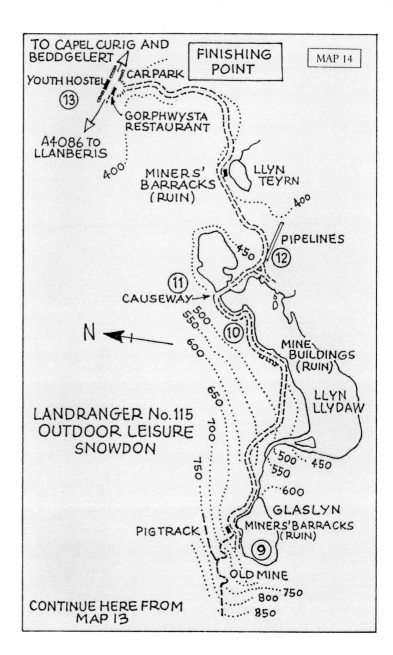

TO CAPEL CURIG AND
BEDDGELERT
YOUTH HOSTEL · CAR PARK
⑬

FINISHING
POINT

MAP 14

GORPHWYSTA
RESTAURANT

A4086 TO
LLANBERIS

400

MINERS'
BARRACKS
(RUIN)

LLYN
TEYRN

400

PIPELINES

450 ⑫

⑪
CAUSEWAY→

N ←

500
550
600

⑩

MINE
BUILDINGS
(RUIN)

LANDRANGER No.115
OUTDOOR LEISURE
SNOWDON

650

700

LLYN
LLYDAW

750

500 450
550

600

PIGTRACK

GLASLYN
MINERS' BARRACKS
(RUIN)

⑨

OLD MINE

800 750

CONTINUE HERE FROM
MAP 13

850

in 1966, because of its immense interest both for its geology
and for its natural history. Access is allowed throughout the
area, but care should be taken not to damage any rocks,
plants, boundary or enclosure fences, etc., within the area.

3 *Erosion — the Snowdon Management Scheme*

It was estimated that in 1975, a typical year, no less than
350,000 people visited the summit of Snowdon, of whom
probably about two-thirds were walkers using the established
footpaths. It is scarcely surprising therefore, that this resulted
in a serious erosion problem on Snowdon, even though a

large amount of work had already been put in to deal with it. It was also a problem that was going to become worse in the future, rather than better, as walking increased in popularity.

It was against this background that the Snowdonia National Park Authority and the Countryside Commission agreed in October 1977 on a five-year programme of work to improve the state of the footpaths and the general environment of Snowdon, and to increase facilities for visitors to the mountain. This initial programme has now been completed, but work still continues both on new projects and on regular maintenance, as it would make little sense to restore paths only to let them deteriorate again.

The main aim of this work is to protect the mountain from the people rather than the people from the mountain. Inevitably, because of the severe weather conditions prevailing for much of the year, a great deal of the work is carried out in the summer months when most holidaymakers are also there. The work, therefore, is a feature of Snowdon that visitors are very likely to see.

The methods for restoring paths have been worked out and well-tried over the years. Slabs of slate dug in vertically across a path and steps constructed from large rocks considerably reduce the surface slippage of material. Once slippage has been prevented, the surface can then be restored with smaller stones or gravel. Ditches dug alongside the path help to remove surface water, while short stretches of fence placed at strategic points discourage visitors from cutting corners or widening paths.

4 *Hafod y Llan Quarry (South Snowdon Slate Quarry)*
The Watkin Path passes close to the buildings and workings of the South Snowdon Slate Quarry, which was active from 1840 to about 1880. The dressed slate was carried by tramway down to Bethania at Nant Gwynant and from there to Porthmadog, by cart. The poor quality of the slate, the high proportion of waste and the high cost of transport were all factors that contributed to the short life of the quarry. The cutting for the tramway, the quarrymen's barracks, workshops, the manager's house (Plas Cwm Llan), spoil heaps and the quarries can all be seen from the path. The bullet holes on the far wall of the manager's house as you reach it were made by soldiers who trained in this area during World War II.

5 *The Gladstone Rock*
The granite tablet cemented into place on the low rock records, in Welsh and English:

'Sep. 13th 1892 — Upon this rock the Right Honourable W. E. Gladstone, M.P. when Prime Minister for the fourth time and 83 years old addressed the people of Eryri upon justice to Wales. The multitude sang Cymric hymns and 'The Land of My Fathers'. Publicly dedicated by Sir Edward and Lady Watkin June 1893'.

The occasion was the opening of the Watkin Path to the summit of Snowdon.

6 *Yr Wyddfa*

The highest point of the Snowdon massif is Yr Wyddfa, at 3559 ft (1085 m) the highest in England and Wales. It is said to be the grave of Rhita Gawr (or Fawr), a Welsh giant slain by King Arthur; hence the English meaning of its name, 'burial place'.

7 *The Summit Hotel*

There have been buildings on the summit of Snowdon for over 150 years, since 1820 when a small hut was constructed from local stone. This hut and subsequent buildings were maintained by professional guides who catered for the many visitors climbing the mountain from Llanberis.

The first Summit Hotel, owned by the Railway Company, was built in 1897. The present building was constructed in 1934 and offered beds and meals until the end of 1942, when it was occupied by the Air Ministry, and the Admiralty and War Department in turn, for secret development work. At present the building is open from late spring to early October for light refreshments; out of season it is heavily shuttered against intruders. It was purchased by the Snowdonia National Park Authority in 1983, although the catering arrangements are continued by the Snowdon Mountain Railway Company. The building was re-opened in 1988 after being completely refurbished inside and out.

8 *The Snowdon Mountain Railway*

The summit of Snowdon is visited by more people than any other mountain in the British Isles. This has been the case for longer than most would imagine. The commercial attractions of a mountain railway were quickly realized and in 1894 construction of the railway begun and was completed in about fourteen months.

The public opening on Easter Monday, 1896 was unfortunately marred by the only major accident — and fatality — to occur on the line. Two trains, one following soon after the other along the same track, had safely reached the summit. On the descent, however, the leading engine mounted the track and ran out of control, eventually leaving the track at a bend and crashing down the steep slopes of the mountain — to the immense discomfiture of several walkers and a climber, who had the unique experience of observing the passage of the engine at close quarters. The second train, unaware of the accident, crashed into the back of the stationary carriages, fortunately now empty. Incredibly, there was only one death — a passenger who leapt from the moving coach and broke his legs. He later died in hospital from his injuries.

Today seven steam and two diesel locomotives are used, pushing single carriage up the 4¾ miles (7.5 km) of single track from Llanberis to the top of Yr Wyddfa.

9 *The Brittania Copper Mine*

The Brittania Copper Mine was working from about 1810 and probably earlier, to 1926. The actual mine is to the right as you descend to Glaslyn down the Miners' Track; the buildings on the shore of Glaslyn were miners' barracks as were those on the shore of Llyn Teyrn; the crushing plant was in the large building on the shore of Llyn Llydaw; both the Miners' Track and the causeway were constructed to enable ore to be carried down to the valley at Pen-y-Pass.

10 *Moraines and Ice-smoothed Rock in Cwm Dyli*

Signs of the Ice Age in North Wales are very obvious in the cymoedd of Snowdon. At several points along the Miners' Track you will see rock smoothed by the moving ice, and just before the causeway the path skirts around some low hills (moraines) made up from the rock debris of the glacier. The isolated rocks lying about the slopes were once carried on the ice but left behind when the ice retreated.

11 *The Causeway*

The north-east reach of Llyn Llydaw is cut by a causeway which carried the Miners' Track to the northern shore. The history of the causeway is described on a slate slab fixed to a rock wall nearby:

'The Llydaw Causeway. This causeway was built by the Cwmdyle Rock and Green Lake Copper Mining Company under the direction of the mine captain, Thomas Colliver. During its construction the level of the lake was lowered 12 ft and 6000 cubic yards of waste rock from the mine were used to build the embankment. The causeway was first crossed on 13 October, 1853.'

The causeway was restored to its former height by the Park Authority.

12 *The Hydro-electric Power Station of Cwm Dyli*

Two steel pipelines, 30 in (76 cm) in diameter, run from the eastern end of Llyn Llydaw through Cwm Dyli for about $1\frac{1}{4}$ miles (2 km) to a power station situated at the head of Nant Gwynant. The water from Llyn Llydaw, falling through 1100 ft (335 m), builds up a pressure of nearly 500 lb/sq in (3.45 Megapascals) at the bottom end of the pipeline and is used to drive three turbines which supply electricity both locally and to the National Grid.

The power station was built in 1906 from local stone and blends well with its surroundings. Its output of 5 Megawatts is small in comparison with some other power stations in North Wales, but hydro-electricity is cheap and does not involve the burning of valuable irreplaceable fuels. It can also be operational in a very short time, about twenty-five minutes, to meet any sudden increase in demand.

13 *Pen-y-Pass*

The valley roads of North Wales were built in the period between 1805 and 1830, the last important construction being that over the Llanberis Pass to link Capel Curig with Nant Peris. Prior to that, the pass could only be crossed by a rocky path, which, according to James Bransby who visited the area, was 'irregular and rough and full of quagmires'.

A few years after the road was constructed, a small inn was built for the benefit of travellers in a sheltered position at the top of the pass at a height of 1170 ft (357 m). In 1900 the inn was taken over by a great personality, Owen Rawson Owen, who remained its tenant until his death in 1962. The original inn was also replaced by a much larger building, the Gorphwysfa Hotel, at the turn of the century. In the years that followed the hotel became the meeting place of a close group of climbers, mainly from a public school background and led by the famous Geoffrey Winthrop Young, who pioneered routes up the great crags of the district in the first great wave of exploration.

Later its importance declined as climbing clubs acquired their own huts and as a new type of climber, of working class origin, took over the leadership in the hills. It was typical of the times that the Gorphwysfa Hotel became a Youth Hostel in 1967. But, in its day, it made a valuable contribution to Welsh climbing.

3.11

CARNEDD LLEWELYN FROM OGWEN

A magnificent walk over the southern section of the Carneddau Ridge. The walk is long but straightforward except for two sections: the steep rise up to Pen y waun-wen and the longer, steeper and more arduous descent of Penyrole-wen at the end of the day. Undoubtedly one of the finest walks in Snowdonia, which includes three of the 3000 ft (914 m) peaks. Most of this land is owned by the National Trust and is part of the Carneddau Estate.

STARTING AND
FINISHING POINT
Ogwen (115-
649603) on the A5
from Capel Curig
to Bethesda.
LENGTH
11 miles (17.5 km)
ASCENT
3200 ft (975 m)

ROUTE DESCRIPTION (Maps 15–18)

(1) From Ogwen walk along the A5 towards Bethesda; immediately after the bridge go through a stile on the R. The path goes on the L bank of the lake as far as a stile over a wall; from the wall the path rises up the hillside to the L. After the rise, the path contours along the hillside crossing several small streams and heading towards a farmhouse, Tal-y-llyn-Ogwen. Just before the farmhouse rise L to a stile in a wall, turn R and drop down hill to a farm road (white arrows). Turn L and follow the farm road to the A5, at the end passing by a wooden hut and conifers. Cross the road half R and go through a small gate.

Follow the farm road beyond (The Old Road) *(2) (3)* to the first of two farms, Gwern Gof Uchaf. Pass it to the R over stiles. Continue along to the second farm, Gwern-gof Isaf; pass this to the L across a field. Just beyond the farmhouse, the path leads over a small stream, through a gateway and ahead to the R of a wall. In the middle of a small belt of conifers turn L through a white metal gate and follow a lane to the A5. The cottage to the R is Helyg *(4)*.

Turn L along the A5 *(5)* for 400 yards (365 m) and then R through a gate and up a road. Continue along the road *(6)*, rising slowly through further gates with magnificent views — particularly of Tryfan — to the L. Immediately before a sheep-fold, about 400 yards (365 m) from the last gate, where the road swings L, take the path leaving to the R. This continues in

63

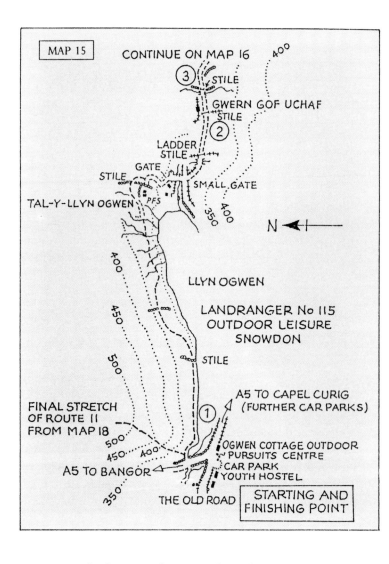

approximately the same direction along the R shore of Ffynnon Llugwy Reservoir; beyond the reservoir rise up a steep slope to reach the top of a ridge at a cairn *(7)*.

Turn L and follow the distinct path along the crest of the narrow ridge, rising eventually to the summit of Carnedd Llewelyn *(8)*. The ridge is narrow at first with a little scrambling but broadens further along beyond the great cliffs of Craig yr Ysfa. From the summit turn L and descend on a faint path to the R of a ruined wall. The path drops to a small col and then continues along the ridge in the same general direction to the summit of Penyrole-wen ($2\frac{3}{4}$ miles, 4.5 km from Carnedd Llewelyn).

To reach the summit of Penyrole-wen, bend L with the path

64

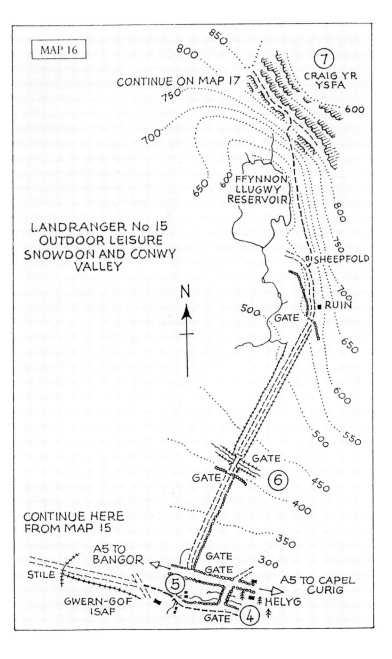

up the final rise keeping to the L side of the ridge, to a cairn which marks the summit. From there it is important to find the best descent point as the summit top is ringed on three sides by very steep slopes and cliffs. Leave the summit to the R from your approach and cross the top, descending slightly to reach a very prominent cairn with stone shelters on the opposite side. From there continue ahead bending slightly L (210° magnetic). After a

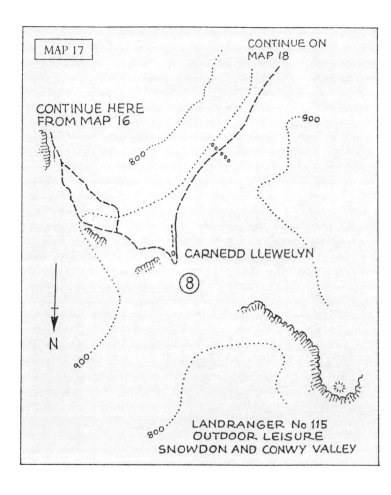

few yards, you should pick up a very faint path which grows more distinct as you descend, keeping to the L of a cliff edge.

The descent of Penyrole-wen is very long and very steep, particularly in its middle section. The rigours of the descent are matched only by those of the long climb in the opposite direction, which is generally acknowledged to be one of the most arduous in all Snowdonia.

Eventually, much later, arrive — probably in a considerably weakened condition — at Ogwen where you started earlier.

1 Aircraft in Snowdonia
Military aircraft are a prominent feature of the Park, particularly around Ogwen and the Nant Ffrancon Valley. These may be UK or NATO aircraft from any of the airfields within the UK as flying time into the Park is relatively short. Many come from the Advanced Fast Jet Training School at

Opposite *Llyn Ogwen*

Royal Air Force Valley, a few miles from Holyhead on Anglesey.

This station was first opened in February 1941 as a base for day and night flights. Today, it is the home of a number of units including 'C' Flight of No. 22 Squadron an operational search and rescue flight, the Search and Rescue Training Unit (SARTU) which trains helicopter pilots, navigators and winchmen to carry out search and rescue duties, and the No. 4 Flying Training School for fast jet pilots. The latter unit has

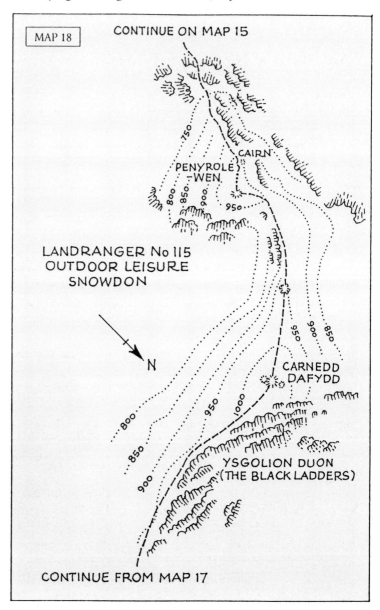

MAP 18

CONTINUE ON MAP 15

CAIRN
PENYROLE
-WEN

LANDRANGER No 115
OUTDOOR LEISURE
SNOWDON

N

CARNEDD
DAFYDD

YSGOLION DUON
(THE BLACK LADDERS)

CONTINUE FROM MAP 17

operated the British Aerospace Hawk T1 since 1976, and these red and white training aircraft may be frequently seen around the Park.

2 The Old Road

The main obstacle to road construction through the Nant Ffrancon Valley lies at the western end of Llyn Ogwen where the Afon Ogwen plunges over a rock cliff over 200 ft (60 m) high. The first road through the valley to surmount this step was built in 1791 by Lord Penrhyn, owner of the Penrhyn Quarry at Bethesda, to reach his lands at Capel Curig with the intention of developing them for the tourist trade. The Penrhyn road was soon supplanted by a turnpike built in 1805 and later by a second and much superior turnpike built by Thomas Telford. The Old Road runs roughly parallel with the present A5 but on the opposite side of the valley and of the Afon Ogwen, remaining reasonably level at around the 725 ft (220 m) contour, to a short distance beyond Pentre where it begins to climb. Its route coincides with that of the A5 around Llyn Ogwen, but from there it again takes a more southerly route on the opposite side of the stream as far as Capel Curig, which it enters over a single span stone bridge over the Afon Llugwy.

3 Telford's Turnpike

The A5, running from Bethesda to Capel Curig through the valley of the Nant Ffrancon and surmounting the steep rise by the Rhaeadr Ogwen at an easy gradient of 1 in 22, stands as a memorial to the genius of one man, Thomas Telford, probably the greatest builder of canals, roads and bridges during the years of the Industrial Revolution.

Telford was born in 1757, the only son of a humble shepherd of the border region of Eskdale in eastern Dumfries and Galloway; when he died in 1834 he was laid to rest among the famous in the nave of Westminster Abbey. The Birmingham and Liverpool Junction Canal, the Caledonian Canal, the Holyhead Road and the bridges at Conwy and over the Menai Straits were but the greatest of his many achievements.

In addition to the road built by Lord Penrhyn up the Nant Ffrancon, a turnpike had been constructed by 1805 to reach the harbour at Holyhead, which serviced the cross-channel boats to Ireland. Although initially successful, shortage of money, both in the building and in the maintenance, soon produced such a deterioration in the state of the road that passage became extremely difficult and at times impossible, and an attempt to run the mail coach along it proved a failure.

Largely as a result of the influence of two Irish Members of Parliament, John Foster, Chancellor of the Irish Exchequer, and later Henry Parnell, member for Queen's County, Telford was commissioned to survey the route. A preliminary report was completed in 1811 and a detailed one in 1817. The work itself lasted for fifteen years, although a through route was established by 1826 with the opening of the bridge over the Menai Straits.

4 *Helyg*

The cottage of Helyg below the cliffs of Gallt yr Ogof about $2\frac{1}{2}$ miles (4 km) out of Capel Curig on the Bangor Road was visited in 1854 by George Borrow who stopped there for a drink of water on a long walk of 34 miles (55 km) from Cerrig-y-Drudion to Bangor, which he covered in a single day. In his book, *Wild Wales, Its People, Language and Scenery*, published in 1862, which has become a classic and still sells well today, he described it as 'a wretched hovel'.

It was derelict and unoccupied when acquired by the Climbers' Club in 1925, opening as a club hut on 30 October. Under the pressure of increasing use it was rebuilt and extended in 1933.

5 *Tryfan from Helyg*

A magnificent view of the east face of Tryfan is obtained from the road by Helyg Cottage. The two objects close together on the summit are often mistaken for climbers, but are in fact two stone blocks about 6 ft (2 m) high, called Adam and Eve. The Heather Terrace lower down the East Face is used by climbers to reach the base of some rock climbs, whilst the usual walkers' route traverses the peak more or less along the skyline of the mountain.

6 *The Leat*

The watercourse crossed about $\frac{1}{2}$ mile (0.8 km) from the road is a man-made leat that diverts water from the high ground above into Llyn Cowlyd. From Llyn Cowlyd the water is taken by pipeline to the power station at Dolgarrog.

7 *Craig yr Ysfa*

A great crag in the Carneddau on the eastern slopes of Carnedd Llewelyn. The crag was late in being explored by rock climbers due to its remote situation, but now has numerous routes. The first climbing hut in Britain was established below the crag in Cwm Eigiau by the Rucksack Club in 1912.

Opposite *View SE from the rise to Ffynnon Llugwy Reservoir*

8 *Carnedd Llewelyn and Carnedd Dafydd*

These are the two highest peaks in the range of mountains between the Nant Ffrancon and the sea, which give the name to the entire range. The peaks are named after Llewelyn the Last who was recognized as Prince of all Wales by the Treaty of Montgomery in 1267 and his brother Dafydd (or David) who attempted to assume that title after his brother's death. Llewelyn was the last native Prince of Wales.

SELECTED WALKS IN THE BRECON BEACONS NATIONAL PARK

*Spectacularly located Carreg Cennen Castle teeters on the edge of a limestone cliff
in the foothills of the Black Mountain*

1·12

THE WATERFALLS WALK

STARTING POINT
Small parking area
on western fringes
of the village of
Penderyn (Outdoor
Leisure Sheet 11/
944089)
FINISHING POINT
Porth yr Ogof car-
park (Outdoor
Leisure Sheet 11/
928124)
LENGTH
3¾ miles (6 km)

'Waterfall Country', as it is known, is a distinctive corner of the
Brecon Beacons National Park. Its shady, thickly wooded
limestone gorges, waterfalls and cave systems are a claus-
trophobic antidote to those wide, open, agoraphobia-producing
spaces which characterize the park. This walk, which follows
the Hepste and Mellte rivers, takes in four magnificent
waterfalls (the highlight of the route is the path that leads
behind one of them). Although quite short, it can be extremely
muddy and, in sections, rough underfoot, so is not really
suitable for very young children.

ROUTE DESCRIPTION (Map 19)

Follow the PFS along the path past the white-painted cottages
and display board which contains a map of the route. Within
300 yards (275 m), where the gravel road turns L, go straight on
over a stile. The path then skirts the rocky outcrops of an old
quarry. Go straight on, following the waymark at the next
junction, where a grassy path drops away half R off the main
track. The path then leads into an open area of rough, rocky
ground. Follow the waymarking arrows as the path runs, more
or less straight on, through the stony ground of these
abandoned quarry workings.

  Beyond the quarry, the terrain suddenly changes completely,
becoming boggy, open moorland. The footpath here can
resemble a black, oozing quagmire, so pick your way
carefully—and make sure that your boots are well water-
proofed. About 300 yards (275 m) after the quarry, cross a small
stream and a stile, following the line of the fence uphill in the
direction of a gate, beyond which there is a sparse forestry
plantation. Bear half R at the gate, keeping the fence to your L as
you walk across elevated, open countryside with panoramic
views north-eastwards to Pen y Fan, to the empty expanses of
Fforest Fawr to the north and, to the west, the open-cast coal
workings around Onllwyn on the edge of the National Park.

Cross the stile by the notice-board warning walkers of the dangerous gorges near the waterfalls and go straight on over another boggy section of moorland between the thinly planted conifers. The path drops gradually downhill towards the thickly wooded, steep-sided gorge in which the Hepste flows, with more spectacular views westwards to the sheer limestone cliffs above the confluence of the Mellte and Hepste.

A scattering of huge boulders, beyond which there is yet another warning sign, marks the point where the path bears R and descends abruptly into the gloomy, craggy gorge by a very steep series of zig-zagging steps cut into the slope. At the bottom is Sgwd yr Eira *(1)* and the most memorable few yards of the walk (especially after heavy rain). This is the section where the path takes advantage of the overhang beneath the waterfall and allows you to walk behind the curtain of water without getting wet (perhaps not strictly true, for the spray can soak you if you linger long enough).

On emerging from beneath the waterfall, follow the indeterminate path downstream for 100 yards (90 m) or so until you come to the series of steps which takes you up and out of the gorge. Turn L at the T-junction at the top of the steep climb and within 15 yards (14 m) turn half R, following the main path up the hill until you come to a conifer-plantation boundary fence. Turn L here, following the path across high ground as it skirts the edge of the forest, passing a fine view-point which looks back down the gorge to Sgwd yr Eira.

The path bears around to the R, still following the line of the forest fence, until you come to a signpost which points downwards to the waterfalls of Sgwd y Pannwr and Sgwd Isaf Clun-gwyn on the Mellte *(2)*. If you wish to see Sgwd y Pannwr at close quarters, then take the path which drops down half L from the main route at this signpost. You will, though, have to retrace your steps back up to the main path after Sgwd y Pannwr, for there is no advised path along the precipitous gorge to Sgwd Isaf Clun-gwyn. (The Brecon Beacons National Park Authority is rightly concerned that walkers should avoid the narrow pathways cut into the near-vertical gorge at this point.)

Having returned to the main 'top' route, follow the line of the forest fence. There are more lofty views along this section, particularly looking back southwards to the Rhigos Mountain, a formidable upland barrier that stands between the National Park and the famous coal-bearing Rhondda Valleys. Above Sgwd Isaf Clun-gwyn, the path bears around to the R, still following the fence (from here there is a spectacular view down into the gorge

Overleaf A path runs behind Sgwd yr Eira, the famous waterfall on the Hepste

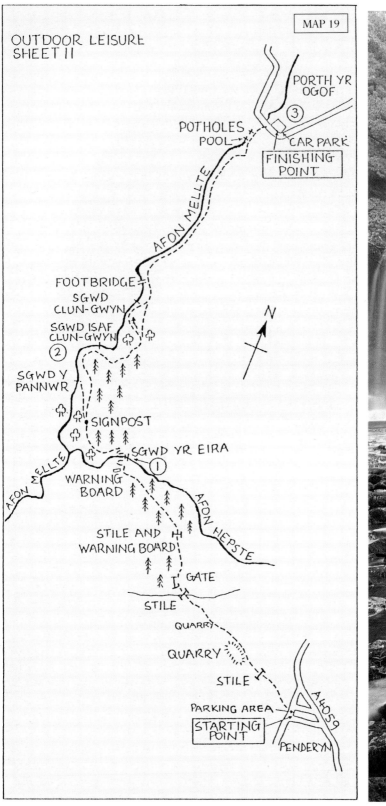

OUTDOOR LEISURE
SHEET II

MAP 19

PORTH YR
OGOF

③

POTHOLES
POOL

CAR PARK

FINISHING
POINT

AFON MELLTE

FOOTBRIDGE
SGWD
CLUN-GWYN

SGWD ISAF
CLUN-GWYN
②

N

SGWD Y
PANNWR

SIGNPOST

SGWD YR EIRA
①

AFON MELLTE

WARNING
BOARD

AFON HEPSTE

STILE AND
WARNING BOARD

GATE

STILE

QUARRY

QUARRY

STILE

PARKING AREA

STARTING
POINT

A4059

PENDERYN

76

as far as the third fall, Sgwd Clun-gwyn).

Continue along the well-defined path. Within 400 yards (375 m) of the view-point, yellow route-markers define the path along the undulating, wooded hillside. At a junction of two paths, bear L downhill, following the yellow waymarks. The path reaches the river just south of Sgwd Clun-gwyn, then runs along the gorge before climbing up beside the waterfall to the high ground above. Make for the edge of the forest.

Within 150 yards (140 m), turn half L and begin to descend again to the river, crossing a rocky section of path. Follow the riverbank past the footbridge across the Mellte, then walk across a grassy field to pick up the riverbank once again. The path then narrows as it crosses rough, boggy ground before skirting the edge of a field and ultimately opening out into a wide, grassy area on the approach to Porth yr Ogof (3).

Leave the riverbank and pick your way across the polished, irregularly shaped limestone rocks above the dark pool where the Mellte emerges from the cave. The path then runs on the ground above the course of the underground river, which can be heard as it flows past two large pot-holes just off the route. At the surfaced road, turn R and immediately L to the Porth yr Ogof car-park. To view the cave, follow the path down into the gorge from the car-park.

1 *Sgwd yr Eira*

Although not the tallest of the waterfalls in this area, Sgwd yr Eira is undoubtedly the most famous. This is probably because the path hugs the ledge directly beneath the overhang, allowing walkers to venture behind the drop of water. In times gone by, this route was much appreciated by local farmers, who used the ledge to drive their flocks across the river. The novelty of seeing a waterfall from the inside out is possible because a 5-ft (1.5 m) band of soft shales, lying beneath a tougher, thicker band of rock above, has been washed away to create a concavity behind the fall. A wide sheet of water drops 50–60 ft (15–18 m) over Sgwd yr Eira ('The spout of snow') on the Hepste.

Another notable feature of this river valley and the neighbouring Mellte is the outstanding natural woodlands which flourish in these limestone gorges. The woods are mostly of oak, with some birch, alder, ash, hazel and rowan.

2 *Sgwd y Pannwr, Sgwd Isaf Clun-gwyn and Sgwd Clun-gwyn*

These three falls are on the Mellte. They appear within less than a mile (1.6 km) of each other, creating a watery staircase in a steep-sided, thickly wooded gorge. The first of the falls on this walk is Sgwd y Pannwr ('The Fall of the Fuller'). Upstream are the two main falls of the river, Sgwd Isaf Clungwyn ('Lower White Meadow Fall')—the curved top of which is said to resemble a 'miniature Niagara'—and Sgwd Clun-gwyn ('White Meadow Fall').

Geologically, these falls signal a change in the underlying rock structure. Sgwd Clun-gwyn stands on the line where millstone grits (to the south) begin to overlay the limestones (to the north). The grits consist of variable bands of rock and shale which offer varying levels of resistance to erosion. Water flows over the harder, upper beds but erodes the softer shales below to produce rapids and, also under the influence of faulting, waterfalls. The best example of this differential erosion can be seen at Sgwd Isaf Clun-gwyn, where a fault has brought hard and soft millstone grits together.

When these falls are in full spate they make a marvellous sight. In the words of one writer, 'To see them in perfection the traveller must wait for rain . . . For this he need not wait long as the country is seldom two days without showers.'

3 *Porth yr Ogof ('Gateway of the cave')*

This awesome cave entrance, probably the largest in Wales, swallows up the Mellte, the river reappearing ¼ mile (400 m) downstream in a deep, dangerous pool. Watercourses come and go with surprising irregularity along this part of the Mellte, often flowing underground, a phenomenon explained by the underlying rock, carboniferous limestone. This easily soluble rock erodes to produce fissures, pot-holes and caverns, the largest of which is Porth yr Ogof.

Today, the cave is a popular venue for parties of pot-holers. When the river is low, you can venture a very short distance into the cave by walking along a natural platform. In the gloom, you should be able to pick out a white formation. This is a band of white calcite in an otherwise black rock wall. Its shape, which resembles a horse, gives the cavern its alternative name of 'White Horse Cave'. Avoid the temptation to explore this dangerous cave system unless you are properly equipped and in the company of experienced cavers.

1·13

CARREG CENNEN AND RIVER LOUGHOR

STARTING AND
FINISHING POINT
Carreg Cennen
Castle car-park
beside Castell Farm
(Outdoor Leisure
Sheet 12/666194)
LENGTH
4½ miles (7 km)
ASCENT
400 ft (120 m)

This attractive circular walk along agricultural lanes and footpaths is suitable for all ages and makes a great half-day out for all the family. The walk descends into the Cennen Valley along a waymarked route through field and meadow to the source of the River Loughor, then returns to Carreg Cennen along an old farm road to the foot of the castle cliff. The final mile (1.6 km) of the walk is mostly uphill through castle woodland, to reach the high limestone crag above. There are several natural and historical features along the way, the most outstanding of which is Carreg Cennen, a spectacular castle complete with dungeon and ancient cave.

ROUTE DESCRIPTION (Map 20)

From the car-park go back along the minor road, then turn L at the first junction and walk downhill into the Cennen Valley for ½ mile (800 m). Cross over a stile in the hedgerow on the R just before Pantyffynnont Cottage, then go straight down across the fields, crossing two further stiles to reach the river. Take care where the path is slippery and steep, just above the water-meadow. Cross over the river by the narrow footbridge (note the novel sheep barrier), walk on to an iron-rail gate, then go uphill along the public path to reach Llwyn-bedw farm. Turn R and follow the stony farm track for ½ mile (800 m) through fields and rough grazing land to ford a stream, then carry on uphill to a junction just beyond a small cattle-grid. Turn L through the open gateway and follow the approximate track to reach a stream and a stone-flag bridge. Look back along the stream's course for a view across fields and woodland to the castle cliff. A solitary heron can often be seen flapping along the Cennen Valley, seeking fishing grounds in the marshy land below.

Walk on, crossing two stiles, then on beside a stream for ¼ mile (400 m) to reach a small enclosure of trees and a stile on the right. This is the source of the River Loughor and the river-

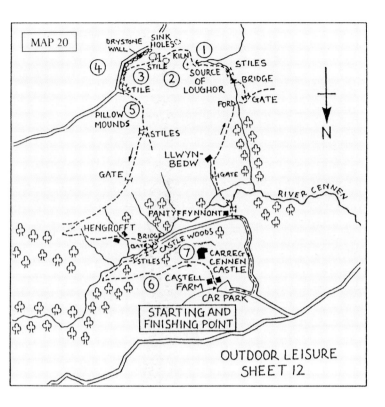

cave and pool can be seen from the high bank above. There is a
short limestone cave system here, reaching into the depths of
the hillside and only accessible to the experienced caver *(1)*.
Continue along the track, bearing R past an old lime kiln with a
limestone quarry behind *(2)*. The kiln was last worked around
the turn of the century, producing burnt lime for local industry.

Just beyond the kiln the track disappears into open grazing
land. Follow the line of the old stone wall to a stile between two
large craters. These are shake holes caused by the ground
collapsing into limestone caverns beneath *(3)*. Several mature
trees growing in these holes indicate that they were formed
some time ago.

Walk straight on to reach a drystone wall at the edge of a
narrow tarmac road. Turn L and go along the line of the wall to
a stile. The open land to your right is the western edge of the
Black Mountain *(4)*, a vast area of wild upland stretching for
many miles to the south and east.

Cross the stile, walk L along the road for 100 yards (90 m)
then turn L again onto a grass track past the ancient Pillow
Mounds *(5)* to a row of trees, where you can glimpse Carreg
Cennen Castle in the distance. Go straight on, crossing a stile, a

Overleaf Dramatic
Carreg Cennen Castle,
perched on its
limestone crag

81

stream and another stile on your R into a field. Walk the length of this open pasture to a gate, a trackway and a National Park sign at the further end. To your L is a magnificent view of the castle and tree-clad slopes of the high limestone cliff.

Follow the directed path on along the hillside, descending by the muddy track toward Hengrofft Farm in the valley below. Walk through the farmyard, then onto the minor road at a bridge across the Cennen. Turn sharp R through a gate and go on beside the river across several small meadows and stiles to join a waymarked path that climbs back half L up through the castle woodland *(6)* to the cliff-top above. On reaching the summit turn L to visit the castle *(7)* or R down the tarmac path, through Castell Farm to the car-park and your starting-point below.

1 Limestone caves

The limestone areas of the National Park are riddled with water-worn cave systems created by natural underground rivers and streams that descend from mountain and moorland heights above. Whole rivers are often swallowed up, disappearing into a cave or pothole, to re-emerge some distance lower down.

2 Old lime kilns

Limestone quarrying was once a major industry in the area and there are a number of disused kilns and quarries hidden away amid the farmland. Limestone had various uses in the local economy, among them providing stone for barns and houses, limestone dust for making cement and render, and, when burnt in kilns, agricultural quick-lime. The nearby quarries on top of the Black Mountain once employed hundreds of local people, making limestone products for both farming and industry.

3 Shake holes

Pits, craters and holes in the ground appear everywhere in limestone country and are caused by a collapse of the millstone-grit layer into the water-eroded caves of the carboniferous limestone below. Shake holes can be enormous, and it is not unknown for whole buildings to disappear swallowed up by the earth.

4 The Black Mountain

Designated as a Remote Area and a Site of Special Scientific Interest, the Black Mountain is one of the last truly wild areas of countryside left in Britain and has several fascinating geographical and geological features. These include extensive limestone pavements on the summit, crevasses which contain alpine plants and the great knife-edged Fan Hir ridge which has been sculpted by glaciation.

5 *Pillow Mounds*

The area of hummocky land known as the Pillow Mounds is thought to be a Bronze Age burial site, dating from about 3000 BC. However, a less romantic explanation suggests that the long low mounds are Victorian rabbit warrens, created in the late nineteenth century as part of the local industry of breeding rabbits for meat.

6 *Castle Woodland*

The steep hillside of Carreg Cennen is clad with self-seeded oak woodland. Over the years many good trees have fallen owing to the steep, unstable ground and others have died of disease and old age. Because of constant grazing by sheep, there are no saplings to replace the declining tree stock and it seems that the woodland of Carreg Cennen is doomed to disappear unless a management scheme can be agreed.

7 *Carreg Cennen Castle*

Built on a natural 300-ft (90 m) limestone crag above the Cennen Valley, the main structure and defences of the castle were erected during the great thirteenth-century building boom, under the victorious English king, Edward I. Many castles were built all over Wales to consolidate English rule and Carreg Cennen was a key stronghold in the local area of South Wales. The Earl of Hereford and John Gifford constructed most of the major fortifications, adding various towers and employing defensive ideas borrowed from the great castles of Europe.

The castle has passed through several sieges and periods of destruction, having been attacked and taken by various Welsh and English armies over the centuries. Its captors include Llywelyn the Prince of Wales and the last great Welsh national leader, Owain Glyndŵr. The castle was partly demolished in 1462 to render it unusable by local bandits, who plagued the countryside at that time.

Carreg Cennen is one of the great historic spectacles of Wales. Its location—it teeters on a sheer cliff in the foothills of the Black Mountain—is unforgettable. There is even spectacle beneath the ground here. A narrow passageway cut into the cliff leads to a cave-like dungeon and a natural tunnel, where the bones of four Stone Age skeletons (two adults and two children) were discovered. A torch and guidebook are available from Castell Farm tea-shop.

2·14

THE SUGAR LOAF

This is a difficult walk to categorize. On the face of it, it seems better off among the Grade 1 routes. However, its Grade 2 classification is earned by the complexities of route-finding on this mountain. Not that you will fail to find any well-defined paths to the top of this bulky peak, which dominates the Usk Valley around Abergavenny. On the contrary, the problem comes from the wealth of footpaths along the flanks of the Sugar Loaf's grassy, open uplands. Footpaths, trackways, sheep-paths and pony-trekking trails (not all of them marked on the 1:50 000 OS map) criss-cross and interlink, creating a confusing series of junctions and a maze of options.

'I was told to follow the path to the summit; but which path?' is the question commonly asked by puzzled walkers on the Sugar Loaf. On a clear day, the problem is much less acute; with the summit in view, you will get to the top, probably on your chosen route. But on a misty day, navigation is much more difficult among this spider's web of trackways.

Scenically, this walk is outstandingly attractive. The views are spectacular even from the car-park at the starting-point, and they get better and better all the way to the summit.

STARTING AND
FINISHING POINT
Car-park on the
southern approach
to the summit,
signposted off the
A40 on the western
outskirts of
Abergavenny
(Outdoor Leisure
Sheet 13/268167)
LENGTH
4 miles (6.5 km)
ASCENT
825 ft (250 m)

ROUTE DESCRIPTION (Map 21)

From the car-park *(1)*, take the path past the National Trust plinth for the summit. The grassy flanks of the Sugar Loaf are eroded here to reveal the distinctive sandy-red soils of the Brecon Beacons' old red sandstone rocks. After just over ⅓ mile (0.5 km) the path joins a tumbledown drystone wall (on the L). At this point, there is a fork in the path. Bear L along the grassy track that runs close to the wall (the first of the many confusing junctions referred to earlier).

For the next ⅓ mile (0.5 km), stay on the path as it follows the drystone wall. At the point along the path where the wall begins to drop gently down the hillside, keep straight on along the main footpath (a secondary path follows the wall downhill).

85

From here, the path is well defined as it cuts a grassy corridor through the ferns and bracken.

Just over ⅓ mile (0.5 km) after the path has left the drystone wall, you will reach a meeting of tracks, at the point where the route begins to ascend to the summit (until now, the path has been quite level). If you abide by the OS map here you turn R, and within 150 yards (140 m) turn L at a low earth bank and gully running up the mountainside. You can, in effect, go straight on instead of turning R and come to the earth bank a little farther up the slope—see 'cross-path' on the map.

On the approach to the summit, the bank peters out and the path becomes less well marked as it weaves its way among a scattering of boulders and outcropping rocks. The Sugar Loaf summit (2) is a very popular place on a clear day, and even in misty conditions attracts a fair share of enthusiasts who have to make do with picturing the view in their mind's eye.

Descend from the summit in a south-easterly direction (not by the stone staircase which connects with a path leading north-east). The route is initially indeterminate as it picks its way down a steep slope among the heather and the boulders, though on a clear day you should be able to see the intended path farther down the slope. The first real landmark is the mossy, boggy hollow (on the L) which is the source of a spring.

The path, which follows the line of the spring as it flows down a deep gully, becomes well defined as it cuts through the ferns, crossing the stream in its lower reaches. Just under ¼ mile (0.4 km) after the stream crossing, turn back half R at a cross-path to follow a wide, grassy track which skirts the side of the mountain. Go straight on at the next cross-path, and within ¼ mile (0.4 km) bear half L at the junction, walking in a south-westerly direction.

At the next junction, a wide, open meeting of the ways, go straight on. Within ¼ mile (0.4 km), go straight on again at another little cross-path and shortly rejoin the outward leg of the route (by the drystone wall) to retrace your steps to the car-park.

1 View-point at car-park
Many visitors are attracted to this wonderfully located car-park, which stands at 1132 ft (345 m) on Mynydd Llanwenarth on the southern and western shoulders of the Sugar Loaf. The land drops away abruptly into the Usk Valley, the river snaking in a lazy loop directly below. The Automobile Association has erected here an orientation pillar

Opposite *There are huge vistas in all directions from the Sugar Loaf summit*

86

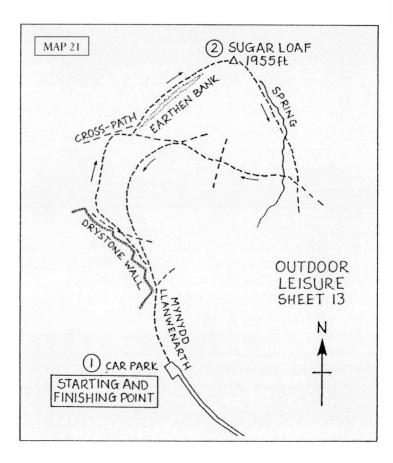

MAP 21

② SUGAR LOAF
△ 1955 ft

CROSS-PATH
EARTHEN BANK
SPRING

DRYSTONE WALL

MYNYDD LLANWENARTH

① CAR PARK

STARTING AND
FINISHING POINT

OUTDOOR
LEISURE
SHEET 13

N

which identifies many landmarks, including the summit of
Blorenge directly opposite, Mynydd Llangatwg 4½ miles
(7 km) away, and the peak of Waen-Rhyd (or Waen-rydd),
12½ miles (20 km) distant.

2 *Sugar Loaf summit*
The views from here are, of course, even better. The north-
western face, shaped like the prow of a ship, looks out across
the pastoral Usk Valley towards the heart of the National
Park, while to the north and north-east the landscape is
dominated by the Black Mountains, which run along the
Wales–England border. A geologically interesting landmark
can be seen 4 miles (6.5 km) to the north-west. This is the
peak of Pen Cerrig-calch (2302 ft/700 m), a limestone
outcrop surrounded by sandstones. It is the isolated, final
remnant of the band of carboniferous limestone rocks which
are found along the southern rim of the National Park, *calch*
being the Welsh for lime.

The Sugar Loaf was presented to the National Trust in
1936, partly in commemoration of the Jubilee of King
George V.

2·15

LLANTHONY VALLEY AND OFFA'S DYKE PATH

The Vale of Ewyas, also known as the Llanthony Valley, stretches for many miles up into the very heart of the Black Mountains. This steep-sided valley has many historical associations reaching back to the Dark Ages and the early Celtic Church, including a connection with the legendary St David, Patron Saint of Wales. The long-distance Offa's Dyke Path follows the high ridge above the valley and marks the ancient mountain boundary between England and Wales.

This walk through history starts from the thirteenth-century Llanthony Priory and ascends the steep mountain up to Offa's Dyke Path, then on along the high ridge northwards. The return journey passes The Vision Farm, the source of inspiration for Bruce Chatwin's gripping historical novel *On the Black Hill.*

The route is suitable for most walkers of average ability, and makes a good half-day out for a family with older children.

STARTING AND
FINISHING POINT
Llanthony Priory
car-park (Outdoor
Leisure Sheet 13/
289279)
LENGTH
8½ miles (14 km)
ASCENT
1250 ft (380 m)

ROUTE DESCRIPTION (Map 22)

Go back down the lane from the car-park to a stile and a gate on the R just past the farmhouse. Follow the path around the old garden wall to another stile, which leads onto the meadowland. Go on along the wide track ahead, straight across the field with the priory buildings directly behind you, to reach a stream and a waymark pointing L, with a small sign which reads 'Way to hill'. Look back toward the priory for a view of the romantic old ruins, set amid green fields, with the steep wooded hillside of Craig Ddu behind.

Cross over the waymarked stile, walk uphill to an open gate, then on up the next field, past several dead trees, to a further stile in the top L-hand corner. Go on up steeply to a small paling gate leading onto the open hillside above. Have a brief rest here to look at the view and to catch your breath for the next stage up to the ridge above. As you look south, the whole length of the magnificent Llanthony Valley is laid out below you, with a fine view of the surrounding hills. Wiral Wood to your L has

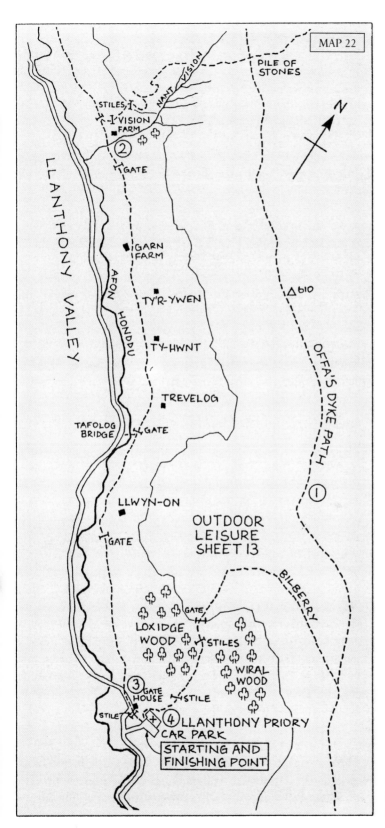

MAP 22

N

PILE OF
STONES

NANT VISION

STILES

VISION
FARM

②

GATE

LLANTHONY VALLEY

AFON HONDDU

GARN
FARM

TY'R-YWEN

TY-HWNT

△ 610

OFFA'S DYKE PATH

TREVELOG

TAFOLOG
BRIDGE

GATE

①

LLWYN-ON

OUTDOOR
LEISURE
SHEET 13

GATE

BILBERRY

GATE

LOXIDGE
WOOD

STILES

WIRAL
WOOD

③ GATE
HOUSE

STILE

STILE

④ LLANTHONY PRIORY
CAR PARK

STARTING AND
FINISHING POINT

Opposite *Llanthony
Priory, an evocative
ruin*

91

suffered some loss of tree cover over the years. To reverse this trend the National Park Authority has taken on a management agreement with the landowner and intends to fill gaps in the woodland canopy by planting young trees.

Go straight uphill toward a clump of thorn bushes, then bear half R, following a narrow path to a group of old box trees. These trees were once part of the front garden of a cottage. Go on uphill steeply toward the rocky summit above, to find a narrow sheep-path heading east through the bilberry, skirting around the top of Cwm Siarpal. Do not go downhill but continue up gently for 1 mile (1.6 km), toward the ridge above.

You will reach a worn track on the flat-topped summit. This is Offa's Dyke Path *(1)*. Turn L and follow the clear trackway northward toward distant Hay Bluff, walking along the Wales–England border for 3 miles (5 km). The level green fields of the Golden Valley in Herefordshire are revealed to your R and due north is the beautiful Black Hill, a high outcrop of the mountains, jutting out into England. The landscape to the L offers a complete contrast, as you look westward across the forbidding uplands of wild Wales.

You will pass several marker stones along the way and an OS obelisk (610). One mile (1.6 km) beyond this obelisk, where the track goes gently uphill, you will come to a rough crossroads, marked 'Pile of Stones' on the map. Turn L along a faint narrow path, walking down the hillside toward The Vision Farm *(2)* in the valley below. The ground is marshy in places and very steep where the Nant Vision plunges down the rocky gorge. Walk downhill to the R of the *nant* (stream), following the public path to the field boundary. Turn R at the boundary, and within a short distance you will come to a stile and a waymarking arrow. Turn L over the stile and walk downhill, keeping the fence line to your L, and in 200 yards (180 m) you will arrive at a second stile (you will now be close to The Vision Farm, which is in private land to your L). Bear half R at this stile, following a waymarking arrow across a field down to the road. Cross a third stile, turning L onto the narrow public road, and go on for 1½ miles (2.5 km).

This little lane is a sheer delight and is reminiscent of what country roads were like before widening and improvement for modern traffic. Go past the small byre, through a gate, then on between variegated hedgerows to pass Garn Farm, a traditional old-fashioned farmhouse complete with tile-stone roof. The Afon Honddu follows the valley bottom to your R and several public paths cross over the river. Ignore all temptation to follow these diversions and continue on along the road. You will come to a sharp R bend just before Tafolog Bridge. Go straight on through the wooden gate, following the trackway through woodland and field for ½ mile (800 m) to reach a further tarmac road at Llwyn-on. The path is boggy in places because of pony-trekking, making bank-hopping necessary. Follow the tarmac to a junction, turn L, go past the pub, then L again at a stile beside a stone barn (3). Go across the field and back to the car-park beside Llanthony Priory (4).

1 *Offa's Dyke Path*
This long-distance path follows, wherever possible, the ancient boundary established in the eighth century by Offa, King of Mercia. Offa's Dyke runs the length of Wales and was the cultural and military divide between the Celts to the west and the Saxons of the West Midlands. The massive earthen dyke, the first official demarcation line between England and Wales, was possibly created to symbolize Offa's power and prestige. There is no dyke on top of the Black Mountains, these forbidding uplands being enough of a barrier in themselves. Along other parts of the border —lower down toward the Bristol Channel, for example—good lengths of the original earth wall and ditch survive surprisingly intact.

Today, the dyke path serves as a pleasurable, if demanding, long-distance walking route for ramblers, stretching for 170 miles (272 km) from Prestatyn in the north to the Severn Estuary near Chepstow in the south.

2 *The Vision Farm*
The author Bruce Chatwin lived at The Vision Farm while researching material for his famous book *On the Black Hill*, now made into a successful film. It is a compelling, meticulously researched history of people and life on the Welsh borders from 1899 up to present times. The farm is not open to the public and walkers are requested not to knock on the door and ask to look around.

3 *Ancient building*
This is the original thirteenth-century gatehouse to Llanthony Priory. The great archway, tall enough to admit a loaded wagon, has been walled up and the building is now used as a barn. The apertures and detailing up above the arch add interest and character.

4 *Llanthony Priory*
St David built his cell here in the sixth century, and his

The Vale of Ewyas is a secluded valley, locked away in the upper reaches of the Black Mountains.

companion the hermit Issui lived nearby up on the hillside, beside the holy well of Patricio. Other solitary monks also lived in the valley during this 'Age of Saints', the golden age of the independent Celtic Church, enjoying the patronage and favour of Brychan, the Irish King of Brecknock (Brecon).

The priory was built much later, between 1175 and 1230, during the reign of Henry II, for the order of Augustinian canons. The building style is Norman and therefore very enduring against the ravages of strife, weather and time. The canons were not hermits, but a teaching order of religious gentlemen with extensive farms and properties in the valley and elsewhere. Constantly plagued by invading mountain bandits, the canons were not above defending themselves, and would set about the invaders with staves and swords. A most unorthodox feature of Llanthony is the unique little hotel—noted for its good beer—built into the fabric of this ancient religious site. A full guide to the priory is available, together with secular sustenance, in the hotel bar.

3·16

FOOTHILLS OF THE BLACK MOUNTAIN

This is a fairly demanding walk into the wilderness area of the remote Black Mountain. The walk starts from the Youth Hostel at Llanddeusant, following old farm lanes to reach the open hill above. It then changes to mountain track, to find and follow the River Usk, which flows down to Pont 'ar Wysg and the Glasfynydd Forest. The return journey across the beautiful hills of Fedw Fawr passes Arhosfa'r Roman Camp and descends into the intricate old footpaths of the Afon Llechach Valley. You will be exposed to the full force of wind and rain during bad weather and a compass is essential for navigation on the open mountain.

STARTING AND FINISHING POINT
Llanddeusant Youth Hostel car-park
(Outdoor Leisure Sheet 12/776245)
LENGTH
10½ miles (17 km)
ASCENT
600 ft (190 m)

ROUTE DESCRIPTION (Maps 23–25)

From the Youth Hostel car-park walk past the village's fourteenth-century church to the junction. Follow the road signposted Llyn y Fan for 250 yards (225 m) to a stile and farm track on the L. Walk up this old lane for ¼ mile (400 m), turn R at the waymarker post and continue uphill to reach the mountain gate at Pen Tyle. The rough mountain track ahead is one of the old Coffin Routes (1) and leads right over the mountain to the industrial valleys of South Wales. Climb up the steep hill ahead, following the rutted path due east above the magnificent Afon Sawdde Valley (2) for 1½ miles (2.5 km), crossing several stream courses to reach a gap in the hills below Bryn Mawr. The path divides here, near the valley bottom. Take the L fork and continue on a bearing of 60° magnetic for ½ mile (800 m) to find the glacial cutting of the River Usk flowing down from Fan Foel above. This appears as a broad, shallow valley with the river following a zig-zag course across the flat, stony floor. Look for a narrow sheep-path on the high L-hand bank and follow the Usk Valley for 1½ miles (2.5 km) on a bearing of 20°, to reach the bridge and tarmac road at Pont 'ar Wysg beside Glasfynydd Forest.

Cross the road, continuing along the L bank of the river to find a stile into the forestry land. Go across the water-meadow,

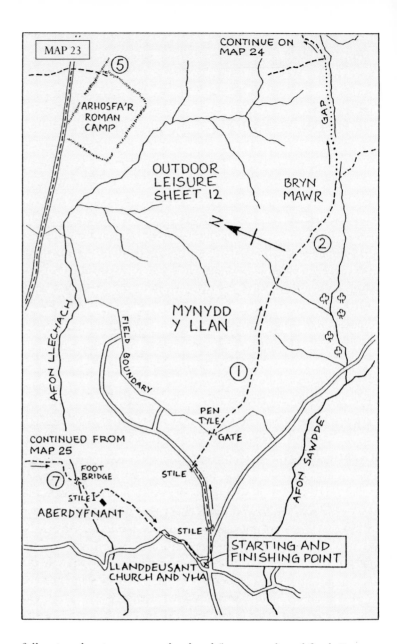

following the river, to reach a hard forest track and ford. Do not cross the ford but go on over the meadowland to climb the high bank on the far side. The river enters the Usk Reservoir by a deep-cut channel below. For a sight of the reservoir and channel continue along the line of trees for 500 yards (450 m). Return by the same route. On returning to the forest road turn R.

Follow the forest road around the reservoir for 1 mile (1.6 km) to reach the far western end, where the open moorland of Fedw Fawr stretches south-west for ½ mile (800 m) to the deep gorge *(3)* of the Afon Clydach. Climb over the stile onto the moorland and walk along the valley bottom on a bearing of

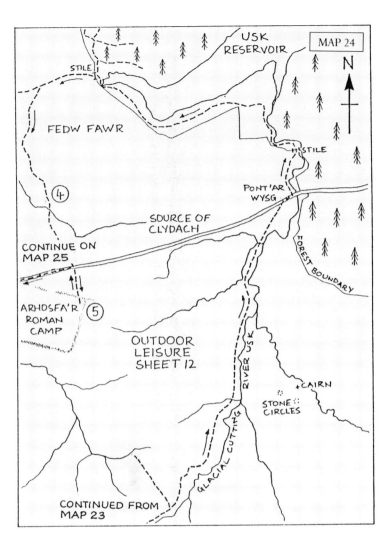

250° magnetic, avoiding the lower marshy ground to find a well-defined path above the gorge. Turn L and go south along the rough moorland track for 1 mile (1.6 km) to reach the tarmac mountain road. This is the best part of the walk for mountain scenery, with the whole length of the Carmarthen Fans (4) visible ahead.

The faint outline of Arhosfa'r Roman marching camp (5) can be found on the hill above the road. Walk straight uphill, looking for a line of very low earthworks at the sharp north-east corner of the camp. Return by the same route. Follow the tarmac road westward (i.e., to the L after returning), cross the cattle grid and walk on for 1 mile (1.6 km) to the attractive Blue Chapel (6) at Talsarn. Just beyond the chapel on the same side of the road is a gate and entrance to an old public road. Walk down this narrow sunken path into the valley, keeping R at the first junction, to reach a field and track just beyond a makeshift

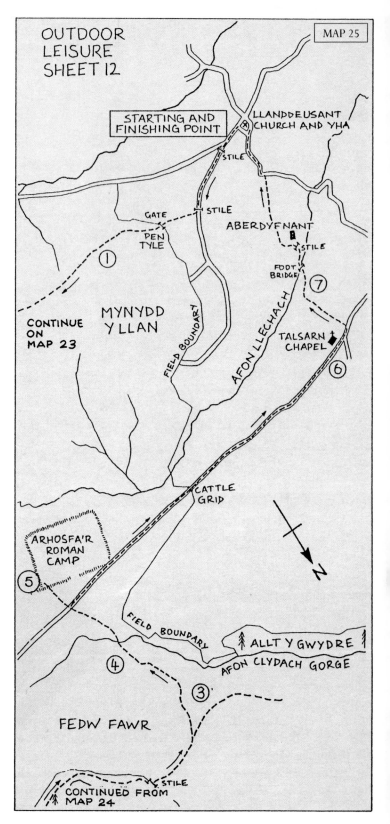

OUTDOOR
LEISURE
SHEET 12

MAP 25

STARTING AND
FINISHING POINT

LLANDDEUSANT
CHURCH AND YHA

STILE

GATE
STILE

ABERDYFNANT

PEN
TYLE

STILE

①

FOOT
BRIDGE

⑦

MYNYDD
Y LLAN

FIELD BOUNDARY

AFON LLECHACH

TALSARN
CHAPEL

CONTINUE
ON
MAP 23

⑥

CATTLE
GRID

N

ARHOSFA'R
ROMAN
CAMP

⑤

FIELD BOUNDARY

ALLT Y GWYDRE

④

AFON CLYDACH GORGE

③

FEDW FAWR

STILE

CONTINUED FROM
MAP 24

Opposite *The bulky,
bare Black Mountain
from Mynydd y Llan*

gate. Turn R, follow the overgrown lane downhill to a stile and a bridge over the beautiful wooded gorge of the Afon Llechach *(7)*. Cross the river, walk on to the working farm of Aberdyfnant, bearing L at the farmhouse, to follow the hard lane steeply up, then carry on for ½ mile (800 km) to the tarmac minor road. Turn L and continue for a further ½ mile (800 m) along the road to the Llanddeusant Church and Youth Hostel.

1 *Coffin Routes*
   The Industrial Revolution of the nineteenth century brought about a migration of labour from the rural areas to the new mines and quarries in South Wales. Dangerous working conditions caused many deaths among the workforce, which made necessary the regular conveyance of the dead back over the mountain for burial in Llanddeusant or Gwynfe. The rough tracks known as 'coffin routes' came into use, and the gambo-cart, a two wheeled vehicle pulled by a horse and the dead man's workmates, transported the coffin. There is a flat area at the half-way point, just below the summit of Fan Brycheiniog, where a short religious service was held before the coffin was handed over to mourning relatives.

2 *Afon Sawdde Valley*
   This deep-cloven valley winds up into the hills to the source of the Afon Sawdde at Llyn y Fan Fach, a small glacial lake at the foot of Bannau Sir Gaer. The great cliffs of the old red sandstone escarpment dominate the skyline, towering above the lake and valley. This landscape is truly primeval and has changed little since rivers of ice shaped the hills and valley during the last Ice Age. The fields and small farms in the valley bottom date from the Middle Ages, and the field pattern remains largely unaltered since the Victorian period.

3 *Afon Clydach gorge*
   Of all the streams and rivers that descend from the Black Mountain, the Afon Clydach is the most dramatic. The stream rises on the moorland of Fedw Fawr and plunges down into the deep, winding gorge, heading north-west through the wooded hills to join the Afon Bran near Myddfai.

4 *Carmarthen Fans*
   Walking south above the Clydach Gorge reveals a whole panorama. In front looms the high wilderness of the Black Mountain, stretching up to the Carmarthen Fans. This mountain range is the western end of the great old red sandstone escarpment and marks the historical boundary of the ancient Kingdom of Brecknock.

5 *Roman marching camp*

This square earthwork was made nearly 2000 years ago by a Roman legion while on the long march west to Carmarthenshire. The low walls, sunk to almost nothing over the centuries, were dug by the troopers in one evening before they settled down for the night. The camp would probably have been used by other marching columns and may have been a regular stopping point on this stretch of Roman road.

6 *Talsarn Chapel*

The tiny Blue Capel (chapel) at Talsarn is one of many independent Methodist meeting houses built during the nineteenth-century revival of the movement. Methodism was quite a political force in its heyday, attracting a majority of the local population away from the Anglican Church. Many chapel members refused to pay the hated Church Tithe, levied on every family in the parish as the dues and living of the incumbent vicar. This popular dissent was later ratified in Parliament by the disestablishment of the Anglican Church in Wales and the subsequent abolition of the vicar's tithe. The present congregation is reduced to a handful of local farmers supporting the chapel out of their own resources.

7 *The old lanes*

These old agricultural lanes and paths are the remains of the nineteenth-century road system connecting farm dwellings. Parts of this Victorian infrastructure are still in regular use today for the passage of sheep and cattle.

The empty moors near Pont'ar Wysg

101

3·17

THREE PEAKS

STARTING AND
FINISHING POINT
Parking area at
Cwm Llwch
camping ground
(Outdoor Leisure
Sheet 11/006245)
LENGTH
9 miles (14 km)
ASCENT
2000 ft (610 m)

The famous peaks of the Brecon Beacons—Pen y Fan, Corn Du and Cribyn—dominate the mountain skyline and are the main objectives for most visitors to the National Park. The most popular route up to the summits from Storey Arms is known as the tourist route. This is best avoided by the serious walker on the grounds of both credibility and conservation, for the wear and tear on this track is already considerable.

A less-damaged and much more interesting linear walk to the tops starts from the woodland camping ground at Cwm Llwch. The first half of the walk is continually uphill, and although the ascent is gentle at first, it can come as a nasty shock to the inexperienced when the serious climb begins up the steep face of Craig Cwm Llwch.

Extra clothing is essential because conditions on the summits are nearly always more extreme than in the temperate lowlands. You should also bear in mind that there is no cover on the open mountain, so that the walker is exposed to the full force of wind and rain during bad weather.

ROUTE DESCRIPTION (Maps 26, 27)

From the parking area go along the rough track, following the course of the Nant Cwm Llwch through tree-lined meadows. Cross over a wooden footbridge by a gate, then go on up the track to reach a sheep pen and a small building beyond. This was once a Youth Hostel but is now a private bothy rented by school and youth groups. Turn R at the waymark and skirt around the former hostel to reach two stiles, rejoining the track for a long climb up past low trees and bushes to a ladder-stile visible at the mountain boundary ahead.

The great vale of Cwm Llwch is laid out before you, with the twin peaks of Pen y Fan and Corn Du towering above; Cribyn, the third summit, is farther east, hidden behind Pen y Fan. The route ahead can be seen from the ladder-stile, leading diagonally up the R-hand side of the *cwm* toward the summit ridge above.

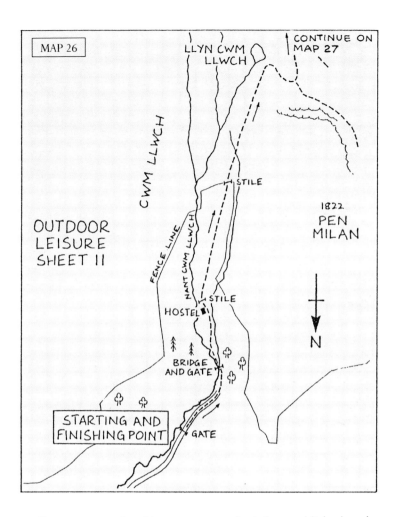

CONTINUE ON MAP 27

MAP 26

LLYN CWM LLWCH

CWM LLWCH

OUTDOOR
LEISURE
SHEET 11

FENCE LINE

NANT CWM LLWCH

STILE

1822
PEN
MILAN

N

STILE

HOSTEL

BRIDGE
AND GATE

STARTING AND
FINISHING POINT

GATE

Walk on past a pile of loose stone to find the established path, which goes steeply uphill for 1 mile (1.6 km).

The small glacial lake of Llyn Cwm Llwch will soon come into view down on your L. It is a good idea to stop at frequent intervals to catch your breath on this steep ascent, and to look around at the mountain landscape. The lake below is held back by a high moraine (earth wall) and was created by a glacier pushing up this wall of earth and stones during the final stages of the last Ice Age. The lake is the puddle of water left by the last of the melted ice.

Turn L at the top and follow the main track along the edge of the escarpment toward the summit of Corn Du ahead. Over to your R, and just hidden from view, is the famous Tommy Jones Obelisk (1), a Victorian monument built in memory of a small boy who died on the Beacons. Go on by the very worn track up to the top of Corn Du, then on across the saddle to Pen Y Fan (2) for splendid views in all directions.

Descend from Pen y Fan on the far side, taking care when

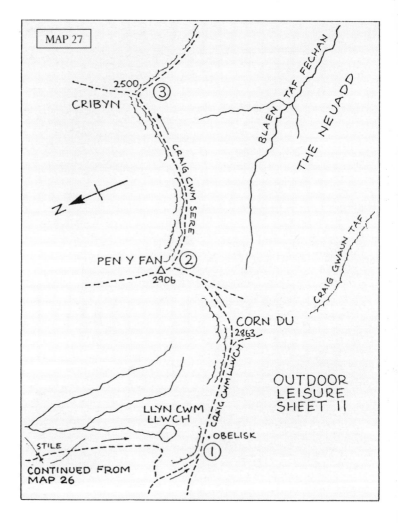

MAP 27

climbing down the steep and slippery path, to join the trackway along Craig Cwm Sere, walking for 1 mile (1.6 km) along the top of the escarpment to Cribyn (3), the summit directly east of Pen y Fan.

Return to Pen y Fan, then go back across the saddle to Corn Du. Follow the path of your outgoing route down the mountainside, passing the Tommy Jones Obelisk and Llyn Cwm Llwch, to reach the ladder-stile at the edge of the farmland. Go on down the track, cross the stiles at the former hostel and return through the meadowland to your starting-point.

1 Tommy Jones Obelisk

The obelisk in memory of Tommy Jones was erected by voluntary subscription to mark the spot where he died in 1900. On the night of 4 August, little Tommy, aged five, lost his way in the dark while walking between Cwmllwch Farm and the Login, straying up the steep mountainside toward the

Opposite The approach to Corn Du from Cwm Llwch

104

summit of the Beacons above. He finally collapsed and died of exposure here on the high ridge above Llyn Cwm Llwch. The people of Brecon searched the area around Cwmllwch Farm for twenty-nine days, not thinking that Tommy could have walked so far up the mountain. A Mr and Mrs Hamer of Castle Madoc near Brecon found Tommy's remains on 2 September, following a dream which Mrs Hamer had telling her of the exact place where his body lay.

2 *Pen y Fan*

This, the highest point of the Brecon Beacons, stands at 2906 ft (886 m), just 43 ft (13 m) taller than neighbouring Corn Du. Both summits have paid the price of popularity and are now seriously eroded by the boots of many thousands of walkers determined to get to the top. A number of suggestions have been put forward to relieve the problem, including making cobble-stone pathways a permanent feature of the mountain summits. The ground is now so damaged that any hard surface would seem an improvement on the present sorry state. However, many purist walkers would disagree, claiming this would limit their personal freedom of the hills and their right to wander.

As you look north across the Usk Valley there are fine views into the heartland of Wales, with the Cambrian uplands clearly visible on the horizon. The view westward looks across the wastes of Fforest Fawr to the Black Mountain and the Fan Hir escarpment. To the south, the long, high ridge of Craig Gwaun Taf snakes its way down to the Taf Fechan Valley beyond. The best view is eastward along the face of the old red sandstone escarpment. The distinctive strata lines of the harder brownstones stand out on the face of Cribyn, and continue along the cliff-face to Fan Big and the eastern headlands of Craig y Fan above the Talybont Valley. This landscape to the east is best viewed in the evening or early morning sun when the shadows and highlights are at their sharpest.

3 *Cribyn*

A delightful summit, Cribyn is often by-passed by the long-distance walker, as there is a lower path on the southern side. The ancient 'gap' road from Cantref to Taf Fechan passes around the steep north-eastern slope, climbing up the west side of Cwm Cynwyn from the Usk Valley to the gap in the hills above the great amphitheatre of the Neuadd.

SELECTED WALKS IN THE PEMBROKESHIRE COAST NATIONAL PARK

Broad Haven's huge beach

1·18

DINAS ISLAND

STARTING AND
FINISHING POINT
Car-park at Cwm-
yr-eglwys
(Pathfinder Sheet
SN 04-14/015401)
LENGTH
3¼ miles (5 km)

This wonderful little walk will take you right around Dinas
Island (an island in name only: it was cut off from the mainland
8000 years ago but is now linked to it by a low-lying valley).
Walkers are rewarded with expansive views eastwards and
westwards along the Pembrokeshire coast, and a glimpse of
teeming bird life. The walk is suitable for all the family, as long
as extra-special care is taken with younger children on certain
sections of the route where the path passes close to abrupt
drops to the sea.

ROUTE DESCRIPTION (Map 28)

From the car-park near the church (1) follow the metalled road
up the hill. Within 150 yards (140 m) turn R at the footbridge,
following the sign for the coast path, and climb up the side of
the thickly wooded and bracken-covered hillside above Cwm-
yr-eglwys. Within about 250 yards (225 m) go over a stile into
open countryside, where you will enjoy magnificent coastal
views eastwards to Cemaes Head and the start of the
Pembrokeshire Coast National Park.

On the approach to Needle Rock (2), the path narrows as the
grassy hillside becomes steeper. Continue past the rock and
climb up a series of steep steps to a stile. For the next ¼ mile
(400 m) or so, the narrow path hugs the cliff-tops, often close to
the edge—so great care should be taken.

Pwll-glas, a huge, black, sea-washed rock, comes into view
and the hillside becomes a little less precipitous. (The latter is
carpeted in a splendid display of bluebells in late spring.) Follow
the path up the flank of the hill to Dinas Island's 463-ft (141 m)
summit of Pen-y-Fan, which stands directly above Dinas Head.
From the OS obelisk, there are more superb views, this time
westwards along the coast right into Fishguard Bay and farther
west again to St David's.

Follow the path downwards along the exposed, west-facing
coast of Dinas Island, for ¼ mile (1.2 km). On the approach to

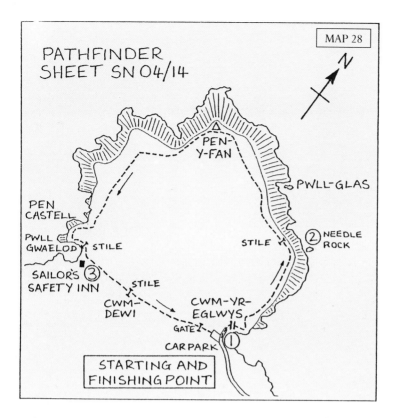

MAP 28

PATHFINDER
SHEET SN 04/14

N

PEN-
Y-FAN

PWLL-GLAS

PEN
CASTELL

PWLL
GWAELOD STILE

STILE

② NEEDLE
ROCK

SAILOR'S ③
SAFETY INN

STILE

CWM-
DEWI

CWM-YR-
EGLWYS

GATE

CAR PARK ①

STARTING AND
FINISHING POINT

Pwll Gwaelod, the path descends abruptly, passing close to the cliff-edge above the shingle cove of Pen Castell before joining the metalled road above the sandy beach at Pwll Gwaelod.

At the stile, turn half R and walk down this metalled road towards the Sailors' Safety Inn (3). Just before the inn, turn L at the PFS and follow the path along the little valley of Cwm-Dewi (a glacial melt-water channel), past marshy ground to the R. Within ¼ mile (400 m) go straight on over a stile. On the approach to Cwm-yr-eglwys, go through the gate and follow the path along the side of a small caravan park next to the car-park, the starting-point of the walk.

1 Cwm-yr-eglwys
The Welsh name of this pretty little village means 'the valley of the church'. Unfortunately, the church, which overlooks the sea, is in poor shape. Only the belfry and part of the west wall remain of this twelfth-century Celtic-style church. It was wrecked by a huge storm in October 1859 which also claimed over 100 ships off the Welsh coast. A religious site may well have been founded here as early as the sixth century, for the church is dedicated to St Brynach, an early Christian missionary from Ireland.

Pwll-glas (in the foreground) and Needle Rock, Dinas Island

2 *Needle Rock*

The path overlooking this angular sea stack is a perfect vantage point for bird-watchers. The rock, a thriving bird colony, is at its busiest between April and July. Herring gulls, razorbills, great black-backed gulls, shags, feral pigeons and guillemots nest on the rock, while fulmars, rock pipits and jackdaws nest on the cliffs just below the path.

3 *Sailors' Safety Inn*

This unusually named inn, which dates back to the late sixteenth century, has always displayed a light at night to help guide ships across Fishguard Bay. It is also one of the few pubs located on the coast path—so make the most of it.

1·19

BROAD HAVEN TO STACKPOLE QUAY

This walk combines spectacle and scenic variety. Stackpole Head is undoubtedly the most impressive feature along the route. The walk also takes in two exceptionally attractive, sandy beaches—Broad Haven and Barafundle—and, on a slight detour, the unusual freshwater lily ponds at Bosherston. The route is easy, but there is the usual proviso concerning the steep Pembrokeshire cliff-top paths and sudden drops to the sea.

STARTING POINT National Trust car-park above Broad Haven beach (Pathfinder Sheet SR 89-99/976938) FINISHING POINT National Trust car-park at Stackpole Quay (Pathfinder Sheet SR 89-99/ 992958) LENGTH 3 miles (5 km)

ROUTE DESCRIPTION (Maps 29, 30)

From the National Trust building at the car-park, pass Stackpole National Nature Reserve information board and follow the path down to Broad Haven beach. Walk along the edge of this attractive, sheltered beach, following the line of the sand dunes. At the northern end of the dunes, bear L along the narrowing stretch of sand leading to the neck of the beach. Then continue along the remainder of the beach, crossing a few boulders on the approach to the narrow strip of land, a barrier between salt-and freshwater, that separates the beach from Bosherston Lakes *(1)*.

At the lakeside signpost here, bear R toward Stackpole Head. (This signpost is also the point of departure from the coast path for those wishing to take a circular walk around the banks of Bosherston Lakes.) Continue on the path and within 100 yards (90 m) ascend a log staircase laid across the fragile dunes, climbing to a grassy headland with good views of the lakes.

Follow the path to Saddle Point, where the angular, towering sea-cliffs of Stackpole Head come into view. Go past a spectacular blowhole on the R (one of the many along South Pembrokeshire's limestone coast), its sea-filled basin sunk deep into the headland. Continue on for ¼ mile (400 m) to the stile above Saddle Bay, a small, sandy, cliff-bound bay with very steep, difficult access.

From the stile, follow the yellow waymarked posts across Stackpole Warren headland (the grassland here is peppered with

111

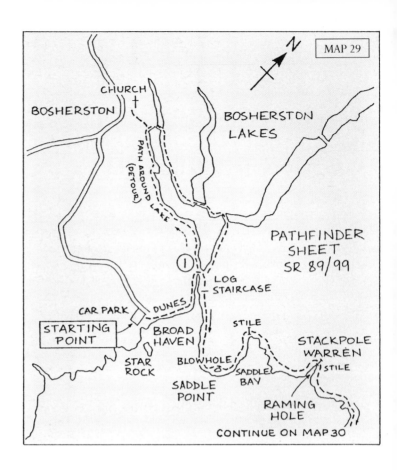

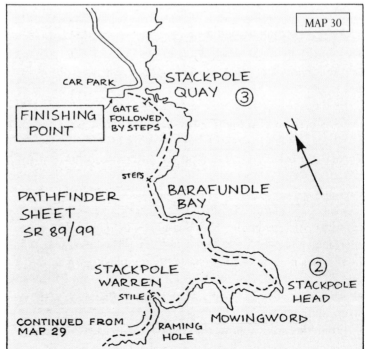

Opposite
*Mowingword
headland, on the
approach to Stackpole
Head*

rabbit holes). These posts come to an end at the stile beside the narrow sea-fissure known as Raming Hole. Turn R here along the path beside the cliffs for Stackpole Head. The path first passes the lesser promontory known as Mowingword before running around the wild, windy and truly spectacular Stackpole Head *(2)*. Take special care on this exposed, precipitous headland, particularly on a gusty day.

Continue on the path for ½ mile (800 m) to the fine view-point (with benches) which overlooks Barafundle Bay, one of Pembrokeshire's prettiest beaches. Go down through the woods to the sands, walk across the beach and ascend a series of steps at its north corner. Beyond the gate and arch at the top of the steps the path crosses a grassy headland on the approach to Stackpole Quay *(3)*. Go through the gate above the quay, turn L at the bottom of the steps and follow the path beside a wall to the car-park.

1 Bosherston Lakes

These lakes are part of the Stackpole National Nature Reserve. They wind their way like three long, thin fingers through the undulating greenery close to Broad Haven beach. It comes as a surprise to discover that the lakes are man-made—the valley was dammed in the late eighteenth century—for they blend in harmoniously with their surroundings. The lakes cover 80 acres (32 hectares), the largest expanse of open water in the National Park. They are surrounded by peaceful woodlands, creating a sheltered haven for a wide variety of birds, including swans, mallard, kingfishers and herons. Most of all, though, these lakes are famous for their splendid waterlilies which are at their best in June (the underlying rock is limestone, creating the non-acidic waters ideal for this attractive aquatic plant).

A lakeside path encircles the western lake (a distance of just over 2 miles/3 km), with access to Bosherston, a pretty little village ranged around its Norman cruciform church.

2 Stackpole Head

This is one of the most spectacular promontories in Pembrokeshire. Stackpole Head juts out into the sea in a south-easterly direction. At its extremity, it narrows into a small platform of land, with shuddering drops into the waters far below. Take care here, especially on a windy day. The limestone cliffs around and about are breeding grounds for razorbills, kittiwakes and guillemots.

3 *Stackpole Quay*

Sheltered, south-facing Broad Haven

With its solid but small stone jetty, Stackpole Quay is a harbour in miniature, reputedly the smallest in Britain. Limestone was quarried locally—the quay is located almost on the geological dividing line between old red sandstone to the east and carboniferous limestone to the west—and shipped out from the harbour.

The quay is part of a large National Trust holding, based on the old Stackpole Estate, for many centuries the home of the earls of Cawdor. The trust's Stackpole acquisitions include the coastline from the quay to Broad Haven and the Bosherston Lakes. Old farm buildings near the quay have been tastefully renovated by the Trust and now serve as self-catering holiday cottages. The Trust's car-park occupies the site of the former limestone quarry.

115

2·20

DALE PENINSULA

STARTING AND
FINISHING POINT
Car park beside
Dale beach
(Pathfinder Sheet
SM 80-90/812058)
LENGTH
7 miles (11.3 km)

The satellite view of Pembrokeshire reveals a giant peninsula. If the camera were to come in closer, it would scan a coastline made up of many smaller peninsulas. Among Pembrokeshire's proliferation of promontories, the Dale Peninsula stands out as something special. Located at the mouth of Milford Haven in the far-flung south-western corner of the park, well away from mainstream tourist traffic, Dale is peaceful and unexplored. Its footpaths do not have the well-trodden look to them that you find in other parts of the park. And Dale's neat, self-contained shape offers the opportunity—rare in Pembrokeshire—of following a circular route.

This walk takes in a variety of splendid coastal scenery—everything from windy, west-facing cliffs to sheltered bays in the calm Haven—and there is the promise of an exceptionally attractive sandy beach on the return leg to placate the younger members of the family. There are many stiles on this walk—far too many to mention individually. The ones mentioned in the text are useful reference points along the route.

ROUTE DESCRIPTION (Maps 31–33)

From the beach, walk west along the one-way system, past the Dale Sailing Company and Post House Hotel. Turn R at the T-junction at the end of the housing estate and within 150 yards (140 m) turn L at the PFS along an unmade road. Within a further 150 yards (140 m) cross a stile, following the PFS, and walk through a field for ¼ mile (400 m) to the stile above Westdale Bay, a west-facing beach popular with surfers.

After the stile turn L along the coast path and climb a series of steps up to Great Castle Head, which has impressive remains of an Iron Age fort *(1)*. This first stretch of the path is well defined though thickly vegetated with tall grasses, gorse, fern, foxgloves, thrift and nettles. Looking east across the narrow neck of the peninsula, you see the somewhat incongruous panorama of Dale's natural beauty set against a background of

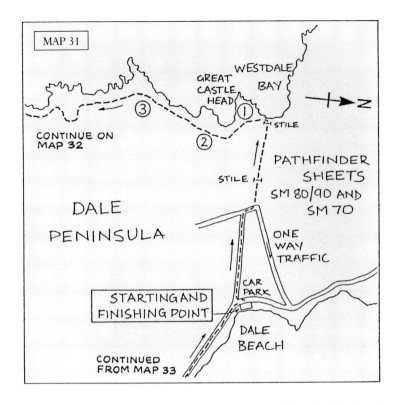

CONTINUE ON MAP 32

PATHFINDER SHEETS SM 80/90 AND SM 70

DALE PENINSULA

ONE WAY TRAFFIC

CAR PARK

STARTING AND FINISHING POINT

DALE BEACH

CONTINUED FROM MAP 33

the oil and petrochemical installations *(2)* that line the banks of the Milford Haven waterway.

The path then runs along the top of the cliff which skirts a rocky, exposed coastline and there are fine views westwards to Skokholm Island and north-westwards along Marloes Sands, past Gateholm Island, to Skomer Island *(3)*. A profusion of wild flowers, including yellow rockrose, thrift, deadly nightshade, campion and bird's-foot trefoil, brings splashes of colour to the cliff-top grasslands at various times of the year.

Go straight on at the signpost for Kete car-park. The path then runs along the top of the craggy, inaccessible Frenchman's Bay. The cliffs are loose, steep and close to the path at this point, so do not stray off the designated route. At the stile just beyond the rock-bound indentation with the unappealing but unforgettable name of The Vomit, turn R along a metalled road for St Ann's Head at the mouth of Milford Haven *(4)*.

Go past the coastguard station and marine rescue centre *(5)*. Turn L at the gate across the road on the approach to the lighthouse and follow the line of the fence (there is no public access to the lighthouse) which runs alongside the road and then beside a row of houses. At the end of the row, turn L and follow the path across a field. Within 250 yards (225 m), the path runs alongside the wall of some old allotments. Bear half L at the end of the wall signposted 'coast path' and shortly cross a stile.

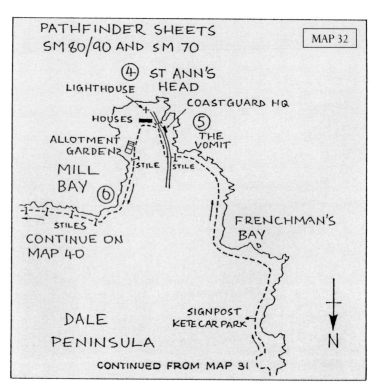

MAP 32

PATHFINDER SHEETS
SM 80/90 AND SM 70

④ ST ANN'S HEAD
LIGHTHOUSE
COASTGUARD HQ
HOUSES
⑤
ALLOTMENT
GARDEN
THE VOMIT
STILE STILE
MILL
BAY
⑥
STILES
CONTINUE ON
MAP 40

FRENCHMAN'S
BAY

DALE
PENINSULA

SIGNPOST
KETE CAR PARK

N

CONTINUED FROM MAP 31

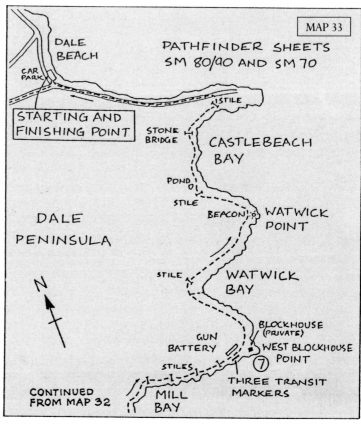

MAP 33

DALE
BEACH

PATHFINDER SHEETS
SM 80/90 AND SM 70

CAR
PARK

STILE

STARTING AND
FINISHING POINT

STONE
BRIDGE

CASTLEBEACH
BAY

POND

STILE

DALE

PENINSULA

BEACON

WATWICK
POINT

N

STILE

WATWICK
BAY

BLOCKHOUSE
(PRIVATE)

GUN
BATTERY

WEST BLOCKHOUSE
POINT

STILES

⑦

CONTINUED
FROM MAP 32

MILL
BAY

THREE TRANSIT
MARKERS

Opposite *Westdale Bay*

118

Continue along the path, dropping down into a dingle from which there is access to Mill Bay *(6)*. Climb back up onto the grassy hill above the bay. For the next ¼ mile (400 m) or so, the well-defined path crosses a number of stiles as it runs along field boundaries near the cliff edge. Cross yet another stile—straight on, signposted 'coast path'—at the western approach to West Blockhouse Point and continue past three tall transit markers for shipping.

Here, the path runs between an abandoned gun battery (on the higher ground) and the Victorian West Blockhouse below (private) *(7)*. Continue for just over ⅓ mile (500 m). At this point you can take a detour R down to the superb, sheltered, golden-sanded beach at Watwick Bay, which is idyllic on a warm summer's day. Rejoin the path and at the stile above the bay turn R along a wide path beside fields to Watwick Point, with its lofty beacon tower.

The path then skirts a field above the pretty, wooded coast which fringes Castlebeach Bay. After you cross a stile, the path drops down almost immediately to an irrigation pond on the L. Within 20 yards (18 m) of the pond, bear half R. Follow the path around the southern stretch of the bay—wooded and bushy in parts, but always well defined—descending to a small shingle-and-sand beach. Cross the stone bridge at the bottom of the steps beside the beach and go back up another series of steps, then follow the path across open headland. Within 100 yards (90 m) of the metalled road, turn L over the stile, then turn L again along the road back to Dale, just over ¾ mile (1.2 km) away.

1 Iron Age fort

Ancient promontory forts are not uncommon along the Pembrokeshire coast. This fine example, dating from about 100 BC, has huge banks and ditches. Its defences also incorporate, quite ingeniously, sudden changes in the level of the land caused by geological faulting.

2 Oil and petrochemicals

Pembrokeshire's coastal harmonies are interrupted by a massively discordant intrusion along the banks of the Milford Haven waterway. Silver stacks pierce the skies above modern jetties and a tangle of feeder pipes which service alien-looking installations where oil is stored and processed. Milford Haven's deep-water channel and the advent of bigger and bigger tankers attracted the major oil companies to its banks. Since the first refinery was opened in 1960, the Haven has grown to become Britain's major oil port, handling some 35 million tons of crude oil and its associated products annually.

Giant supertankers glide in and out of the Haven, the only natural harbour in southern Britain able to accommodate them. Unwelcome though the presence of this industry is in strict environmental terms, we must give due regard to its role in boosting our modern economy. The Haven also enjoys a much-admired anti-oil-pollution record.

3 *Skokholm and Skomer Islands*

Pembrokeshire's sea-bird life is particularly prolific on these two islands. Their strange-sounding names are of Norse origin (as is that of Dale itself, which means 'valley'). Skokholm, the smaller and more remote, was the site of Britain's first bird observatory, established in 1933. Both islands are nature reserves of international repute. Skomer, for example, has one of north-west Europe's finest populations of sea-birds, including shags, razorbills, fulmars, puffins, oystercatchers, kittiwakes, guillemots and an exceptionally large colony of Manx shearwaters. Skomer is the easier island to get to: there are regular boat trips in summer from Martin's Haven near Marloes.

4 *The Milford Haven waterway*

The deep-water Milford Haven has been recognized for centuries as one of the world's finest harbours. Admiral Lord Nelson was one of many to sing its praises as a safe, sheltered anchorage. The Haven is a classic *ria*, or drowned river valley. When Britain's glaciers disappeared, the water level in the Haven increased substantially, turning it into a deep-water inlet. Even at low tide, its waters are over 50 ft (15 m) deep.

5 *St Ann's Head Coastguard Station and Marine Rescue Centre*

This headland guards the mouth of Milford Haven, protecting its waters from the fierce westerly gales that often blow. Wind speeds of over 100 mph (160 km/h) have been recorded here at least five times since 1946, and there are usually over thirty severe gales a year. Also playing a protective role is an extensive coastguard complex, which includes a powerful lighthouse, offices and housing for personnel. This coastguard station, with its sophisticated equipment, is the modern equivalent of the flaming beacon which burned in ages past at St Ann's Head, warning ships of the dangerous reefs at the approach to the Haven.

6 *Mill Bay*

This obscure, rocky little bay witnessed a dramatic episode in the founding of the mighty Tudor dynasty. It was the

121

Frenchman's Bay along Dale's exposed west coast

landing-point, on 7 August 1485, of Harri Tudur, who was shortly to become Henry VII, first of the Tudor monarchs. Harri, a Welshman born at Pembroke Castle, returned from exile in France with an army of 2000 men. After landing in Mill Bay, he marched through Wales to England's Midlands, gathering more support along the way. At Bosworth Field, on 22 August, he achieved a famous victory over Richard III to take the throne of England.

7 *Fortifications along the Haven*

The West Blockhouse is one of the many fortifications and gun emplacements along the waterway. The Haven has been a busy sea route since ancient times. Serious attempts to defend its waters had to wait until the mid-nineteenth century, spurred on by the potential threat which France posed to the naval dockyard at Pembroke Dock. West Blockhouse was one of the series of nine forts and batteries built at this time. Completed in 1857, it had a garrison of 80 men and formed part of the defences of the outer Haven. The fort also saw use during both world wars, but was abandoned in 1950. The gun emplacements can still be visited, though the fort is not accessible to the public.

APPENDICES

ACCESS FOR THE WALKER

It is important to realize at the outset that the designation of a National Park does not change the ownership of the land within it in any way. In the case of the Snowdonia National Park, for example, in 1980, over thirty years after designation, only 0.3% of the land area was actually owned by the Park Authority, and only 30.5% by all 'public' bodies combined, e.g. National Trust, Ministry of Defence, etc. The laws of access and trespass apply just as much to areas of private land within a National Park as to those outside it.

The National Parks and Access to the Countryside Act of 1949 required County Councils in England and Wales to prepare maps which showed all paths over which the public had a right to walk. The final form of the map is referred to as a definitive map and copies are held at the offices of the County Council and District Council and sometimes by the Community Council concerned. The inclusion of a public right-of-way on a definitive map can be taken as proof that such exists. Paths can only be diverted or deleted from a definitive map by the raising of a Diversion Order or an Extinguishment Order respectively. The paths are classified as either footpaths (for walkers only) or bridleways (for walkers, horseriders and cyclists). Those public rights-of-way were included on the now withdrawn 1 inch to 1 mile (1:63 360) Seventh Series, the 1:25 000 Second Series (i.e. Pathfinder), 1:50 000 First and Second Series (i.e. Landranger) and the Outdoor Leisure maps. In Pembrokeshire, walkers benefit from the long-distance right-of-way that exists along the coastal path and in much of the Brecon Beacons access to the common land is by public right-of-way.

In the Snowdonia National Park however, there are considerable areas of land without any public rights-of-way and they do in fact reach only three mountain summits — Yr Wyddfa, Foel grach (almost) and Penygadair. Furthermore, in many cases, public rights-of-way terminate abruptly in strange out-of-the-way spots; this arose, for example, across a boundary where the owners or councils on opposite sides took different views over the existence of a right-of-way.

Fortunately, however, access to large areas is allowed in practice under one or more of the following:

NATIONAL TRUST AREAS
In 1980 the National Trust owned 8.8%, 43,533 acres (18,265 hectares) of the area of the Snowdonia National Park. The Trust policy is to give free access at all times to its open spaces; however, there cannot, of course, be unrestricted access to tenanted farms, young plantations and woods, or certain nature reserves where the preservation of rare fauna and flora is paramount.

FORESTRY COMMISSION FORESTS
Particularly within the Beddgelert, Coed-y-Brenin and Gwydyr forests where walkers are allowed to walk along any paths or forest roads provided, of course, that they behave in a safe and sensible manner.

COURTESY FOOTPATHS
A number of footpaths have, with the landowners' agreement, been opened for public use although not in themselves being legal rights-of-way. The Miners' Track from near the Pen-y-Gwryd Hotel to Ogwen Cottage and the Precipice Walk are in this category.

ACCESS AGREEMENTS
Under the National Parks and Access to the Countryside Act of 1949, National Park Authorities have the power to negotiate Access Agreements with landowners whereby access is

given in return for compensation in the form of a grant. This access may be subject to conditions as appropriate to the area.

Up to end 1985 twenty Access Agreements had been concluded in the Snowdonia National Park.

TRADITION

Walkers have for very many years walked freely in some of the hill and mountain areas of the Snowdonia and Brecon Beacons National Parks with the tacit agreement of the landowners concerned, even though they may have had no legal right to do so. The tolerance shown will vary from farmer to farmer and, in any case, depends for its continuation upon the sensible behaviour of the walkers themselves. Litter, broken glass, ruined walls, unruly dogs, noisy behaviour, etc., are likely to make it more difficult for the next people to go that way.

SAFETY

The routes described in this guide vary considerably in both length and difficulty. Some at least of the easy walks should with reasonable care be safe at any time of the year and under almost any weather conditions; the more difficult walks on the other hand cross some of the wildest and roughest country in Great Britain and should only be attempted by fit walkers who are properly clothed and equipped and have command of the techniques involved in walking, scrambling and route finding.

It cannot be too strongly emphasized that weather and conditions can change very rapidly in mountain areas, during a day, from one part of a mountain to another or as you climb to higher ground. This must be borne in mind when selecting clothing and equipment before a walk. The severity of a walk will also generally be much greater in the winter when snow and ice are lying on the mountain than in the summer months.

The golden rules for safety in mountain and moorland areas (and, to a lesser extent, the easier coastal routes) are:

DO

Carry appropriate clothing and equipment, all of which should be in sound condition.

Carry map and compass and be practised in their use.

Leave a note of your intended route with a responsible person (and keep to it!).

Report your return as soon as possible.

Keep warm, but not overwarm, at all times.

Eat nourishing foods and rest at regular intervals. Avoid becoming exhausted.

Know First Aid and the correct procedure in case of accidents or illness.

Obtain a weather forecast before you start. A weather forecast with a report on ground conditions may be obtained all the year round from Llanberis (01286) 870120. Information boards around Snowdon give this information on winter weekends and in the peak summer season.

DO NOT

Go out on your own unless you are very experienced; three is a good number.

Leave any member of the party behind on the mountain, unless help has to be summoned.

Explore old mine workings, quarries or caves, or climb cliffs (except scrambling ridges).

Attempt routes which are beyond your skill and experience.

A booklet, *Safety on Mountains*, is published by the British Mountaineering Council, Crawford House, Precinct Centre, Booth Street East, Manchester M13 9RZ.

GIVING A GRID REFERENCE

Giving a grid reference is an excellent way of 'pin-pointing' a feature, such as a church or mountain summit, on an Ordnance Survey map.

Grid lines, which are used for this purpose, are shown on the 1:25 000 Outdoor Leisure, 1:25 000 Pathfinder and 1:50 000 Landranger maps produced by the Ordnance Survey; these are the maps most commonly used by walkers. They are the thin blue lines (one kilometre apart) going vertically and horizontally across the map producing a network of small squares. Each line, whether vertical or horizontal, is given a number from 00 to 99, with the sequence repeating itself every 100 lines. The 00 lines are slightly thicker than the others thus producing large squares with sides made up of 100 small squares and thus representing 100 kilometres. Each of these large squares is identified by two letters. The entire network of lines covering the British Isles, excluding Ireland, is called the National Grid.

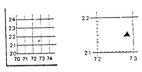

FIGURE 3 Giving a
grid reference

Figure 3 shows a corner of an Ordnance Survey 1:50 000 Landranger map which contains a Youth Hostel. Using this map, the method of determining a grid reference is as follows:

Step 1
Holding the map in the normal upright position, note the number of the 'vertical' grid line to the left of the hostel. This is 72.

Step 2
Now imagine that the space between this grid line and the adjacent one to the right of the hostel is divided into ten equal divisions (the diagram on the right does this for you).

Estimate the number of these 'tenths' that the hostel lies to the right of the left-hand grid line. This is 8. Add this to the number found in Step 1 to make 728.

Step 3
Note the number of the grid line below the hostel and add it on to the number obtained above. This is 21, so that the number becomes 72821.

Step 4
Repeat Step 2 for the space containing the hostel, but now in a vertical direction. The final number to be added is 5, making 728215. This is called a six-figure grid reference. This, coupled with the number or name of the appropriate Landranger or Outdoor Leisure map, will enable the Youth Hostel to be found.

A full grid reference will also include the identification of the appropriate 100 kilometre square of the National Grid; for example, SD 728215. This information is given in the margin of each map.

ADDRESSES OF USEFUL ORGANIZATIONS

Brecknock Naturalists' Trust
c/o Chapel House, Llechfaen, Brecon, Powys
LD3 7SP
Tel: (01874) 8688

Brecon Beacons National Park
7 Glamorgan Street, Brecon, Powys LD3 7DP
Tel: (01874) 4437

Brecon Beacons Mountain Centre
Nr Libanus, Brecon, Powys LD3 8ER
Tel: (01874) 3366

British Trust for Conservation Volunteers
36 St Mary's Street, Wallingford, Oxfordshire
OX10 0EU
Tel: (01491) 824 602

Regional Office, Conservation Volunteers
The Wales Conservation Centre, Forest Farm,
Forest Farm Road, Whitchurch, Cardiff CF4 7JH
Tel: (01222) 626 660

The Camping and Caravanning Club
Greenfields House, Westwood Way, Coventry
CV4 8JH
Tel: (01203) 694 995

Council for National Parks
246 Lavender Hill, London SW11 1LJ
Tel: (0171) 924 4077

The National Trust
36 Queen Anne's Gate, London SW1H 9AS
Tel: (0171) 222 9251

The National Trust
Regional Office for North Wales, Trinity Square,
Llandudno, Gwynedd LL30 2DE
Tel: (01492) 860 123

The National Trust
Regional Office for South Wales, The King's Head,
Llandeilo, Dyfed SA19 6BN
Tel: (01558) 822 800

Nature Conservancy Council
Dyfed-Powys Regional Office, Plas Gogerddan,
Aberystwyth, Dyfed SY23 3EB
Tel: (01970) 828 551

Nature Conservancy Council
North Wales Region, Plas Penrhos,
Ffordd Penrhos, Bangor, Gwynedd LL57 2LQ
Tel: (01248) 370 444

Nature Conservancy Council
South Wales Regional Office, 43 The Parade,
Roath, Cardiff, South Glamorgan CF2 3AB
Tel: (01222) 485 111

Ramblers' Association
1/5 Wandsworth Road, London SW8 2XX
Tel: (0171) 582 6878

Countryside Commission
John Dower House, Crescent Place,
Cheltenham, Gloucestershire GL50 3RA
Tel: (01242) 521 381

Countryside Commission for Wales
Ladywell House, Newtown, Powys SY16 1RD
Tel: (01656) 267 99

Dale Fort Field Centre
Dale, Dyfed
Tel: (016465) 205

Dyfed Archaeological Trust
Old Carmarthen Art College, Church Lane,
Carmarthen, Dyfed
Tel: (01267) 231 667

Dyfed Wildlife Trust
7 Market Street, Haverfordwest, Dyfed
SA61 1NF
Tel: (01437) 5462

Field Studies Council
Orielton Field Centre, Nr Pembroke, Dyfed
Tel: (0164681) 225

Forestry Commission
Victoria House, Victoria Terrace, Aberystwyth,
Dyfed SY23 2DG
Tel: (01970) 612 367

The Long Distance Walkers Association
10 Temple Park Close, Leeds LS15 0JJ
Tel: (01132) 642 205

Snowdonia National Park
Penrhyndeudraeth, Gwynedd LL48 6LS
Tel: (01766) 770 274

The Snowdonia National Park Society
(Cymdeithas Parc Cenedlaethol Eryri), The Ugly
House, Capel Curig, Near Betws-y-Coed,
Gwynedd
Tel: (016904) 234

Wales Tourist Board
PO Box 1, Cardiff, South Glamorgan
CF1 2XN
Tel: (01222) 227 281

Youth Hostels Association (England and Wales)
Trevalyan House, 8 St Stephens Hill, St Albans,
Hertfordshire AL1 2DY

Youth Hostels Association (Regional Office)
1 Cathedral Road, Cardiff CF1 9HA

INDEX

Place names and sites of interest only are included. Page numbers in *italics* refer to illustrations.